KANBAN

SHOP
SIGNS
OF
JAPAN

KANBAN

SHOP SIGNS OF JAPAN

photography and design by
DANA LEVY

commentaries by
LEA SNEIDER

introductory essay by
FRANK B. GIBNEY

WEATHERHILL
New York & Tokyo

Bibliographical Note: The present book has been published to coincide with an exhibition organized by the authors under the sponsorship of the Japan Society of New York and the American Federation of Arts, in association with the Peabody Museum, to tour the United States during the spring of 1983, opening at the Japan House Gallery, New York. The book is issued in three editions: in hard covers, published by Weatherhill for general sale through bookstores; in soft covers, published by the sponsors, and in Japanese, by Tankōsha Publishing Co., Kyoto.

Japanese names prior to the Meiji Period are given in the traditional Japanese style of family name first. Names after the Meiji Restoration are given in the common western style of family name last. The copy editing style used italicizes the first reference to foreign words within each section of the text. Each commentary is treated as a separate text section, since they may be perceived thus by the reader.

Dimensions refer to height × width × depth, and are given in inches and centimeters.

All photographs by DANA LEVY except the following for which the authors give thanks:
YOSHIKAZU HAYASHI, Figures 1, 6, 9, 13, 15, 21, 29, 32, 35, 39
TAJIRŌ MASUDA, Figure 19
TSUMURA JUNTENDŌ, Figure 5
DR. WYNANT DEAN, Plate 76
RANDALL WALLACE, Plate 77
HONOLULU ACADEMY OF ARTS, Plate 101
TAKAHASHI-SHI SHIRYŌKAN, Plate 72

The typeface for the title used on the cover, the title page and for the cap. initials is *Jeune*. It was designed by Doyald Young and this is its first commercial use.

The illustration on the title page depicts a street scene at Nihonbashi in Edo (Tokyo) just before the Meiji Restoration. From "*Nihon no Kanban*" by Yoshikazu Hayashi.

Cover illustration: KANBAN FOR A TEA MERCHANT (Plate 2).

First edition, 1983

Published by John Weatherhill, Inc., of New York and Tokyo, with editorial offices at 7-6-13 Roppongi, Minato-ku, Tokyo 106, Japan. Protected by copyright under terms of the International Copyright Union; all rights reserved. Printed and first published in Japan.

Library of Congress Catalog Card Number: 82-062-648   ISBN: 0-8348-0180-9

CONTENTS

PREFACE

 an may have been a merchant since the beginning of his history, but the
Japanese businessman is legendary. His envied business acumen and his
respected traditions of crafts and graphics have been applied to the symbols
with which he has identified himself as a merchant for five hundred years.

The early prototypes of the contemporary corporate symbol were proscribed by eighth
century laws: *kanban*, sign boards, were required to identify the products sold by merchants at the annual Kyoto fairs. Few signs were produced primarily for aesthetic reasons.
They were utilitarian in their concerns and speak eloquently about the merchants who
commissioned them and the world in which they were used. In their simplest and often
most elegant form, words were not used. An illiterate public could not have read them: a
radish, a string of prayer beads, a vinegar cask, was sufficient to convey the message.

Simple shapes and forms dominate the Edo period when the Tokugawa Shogunate pre-
vailed, but as the merchant class vied with the Emperor for control of his country's destiny
in the Meiji period, the kanban it produced were increasingly lavish and imaginative.
Sumptuary laws enacted by the Shogunate to curtail the extravagance and showy display
of signs—and merchants—were often honored in the breach. The wealth of the merchants
exceeded the wealth of the government and even the Emperor. The balance of power
shifted with the disposition of ready cash in the society.

Lacquer, refined calligraphy, gold and *ukiyo-e* style images were used commonly on signs by
the end of the Tokugawa period. In the early Meiji period, strange new languages and
symbols intruded on kanban as they did on the essence of Japan. As the nation opened her
ports to the bizarre world beyond her shores, signs became gaudier and stranger.

History offers some guidelines for the dating of kanban, but it is an imprecise art. The
styles of calligraphy, the appearance of hitherto unknown products, and the use of trade-

marks give some clues to dates. Trademarks were required by law to be registered in 1884, so signs produced after that date have the mark *tōroku shōhyō*, "registered trademark," or were altered to reflect the new regulations. Periodic efforts by the Emperor to consolidate his power are also reflected on kanban: The use of the Imperial chrysanthemum crest was regulated by Imperial decree.

The images and designs used reflect contemporary sensitivities and symbols. Sumo wrestlers represent strength; *Bijin*—beautiful women who also identify a class of woodblock prints—express pleasure and health; pine trees are symbolic of long life. Japan's penchant for fads is vividly illustrated on signboards. Images of English sea captains, horses and hearts were incorporated into Japanese graphics as soon as they came on the scene. Trademarks were invested with the newest and oddest images. Punning brand names and product identification was an early copywriter's trick, often used.

Signboards are not a traditional art form. Most old signboards were replaced with shiny new metal and neon as they succumbed to the elements or the wreckers. But a few collectors had the foresight to collect kanban from Tokugawa and Meiji period Japan and they show the trademarks of their passion. Kenichi Higasa has built four restaurants in the international port city of Kobe in which he shares his commercial relics with his customers. Gorō Takamura, president of the Shōwa Neon Sign Company, began his collection less than ten years ago as an inspiration to the designers of the neon signs he produces daily. The largest single collection of kanban was assembled by an American and is still in the collection of the Peabody Museum of Salem, Massachusetts. Edward Morse, a marine biologist raised on the coast of Maine and later director of the Peabody Museum, arrived in Japan twenty-five years after Perry's ships. His scientific and aesthetic vision was extended to a collection of nearly two hundred shop signs.

Although virtually all of the designers and carvers of Tokugawa and Meiji period signs are anonymous—and were certainly not considered artists at the time they worked—they have left objects of extraordinary beauty and great significance. Kanban were the inspired creations of merchant Japan and they continue to inspire imitation by the designers and businessmen of contemporary Japan.

LETITIA BURNS O'CONNOR
Editor

KANBAN

SHOP SIGNS OF JAPAN

FIGURE 1. A busy stationery shop is depicted in this Meiji woodblock print. Its stock and trade are symbolized by the account book kanban suspended on bamboo branches from the roof. The calligraphic panel to the right reads, "All kinds of paper goods."

Figure 2. This traditional inn in Takayama utilizes the entire entry to announce its presence. The rough hewn wooden slab affixed to the lintel reads, "for travelling people." It is surmounted by a carved *shishi,* a mythological lion-like beast common in folk art. The name of the inn, Hisadaya, is written on both the paper lantern below the kanban and on the sliding *shōji* door.

Figure 3. *Noren,* a cloth sign like a divided curtain, partially conceals the grill on which this shop prepares *midarashi dango,* sweet dumplings. The name of the product is incorporated in the bold calligraphic design, and the product itself is arranged in a tempting display.

THE MARKS OF A
JAPANESE MERCHANT

FIGURE 4. A law requiring the registration of trademarks was instituted in 1884. Some of the trademarks illustrated opposite are identified legally by the English, "Registered trademark," or by the Japanese, *tōroku shōhyō*.

FIGURE 5. This late Meiji photograph
shows the Tokyo office of Tsumura
Juntendō, manufacturers of Chūjōtō brand
patent medicine. The Heian-style princess, symbol of Chūjōtō medicine, identifies the company on a large contemporary
kanban. See also Plates 71-73.

THE MARKS OF A JAPANESE MERCHANT

by Frank B. Gibney

T HERE IS NOTHING MORE FUNCTIONAL THAN A SIGN. When used in business, the sign's purpose is basic advertising: to attract new customers to a shop, and to remind old customers and their friends that the establishment behind the sign remains both accessible and reliable. The classic Japanese business signs–*kanban*, as they are called–which comprise this exhibition are totally functional in their purpose. Yet the care and style of their execution raise them to the level of art. The art of their design–whether fine calligraphy, ornate gold or silver embellishment, ingenious shapes, or the evocative figures and visual puns they incorporate–testify not merely to the abiding Japanese fascination with form and style, even above content, but with symbol more than substance.

FIGURE 6. This woodblock print, dated 1731, illustrates a Kyoto sake shop that displays a *sakabayashi,* ball of cedar twigs, as its kanban. See also Plate 6.

FIGURE 7. This carved wooden kanban, circa 1630, was hung on an Edo period pharmacy operated by an early generation of the Sumitomo family. The proprietor was forced into the secular life when his Buddhist temple was closed by a rival political force threatened by its influence. Medicine was an appropriate profession since it was both a continuation of the Chinese Buddhist culture and a public service. Sumitomo employees today are shown this sign during their initiation to remind them that public service is still part of the Company credo.

FIGURE 8. The Yono-ya comb shop in the Asakusa section of contemporary Tokyo uses the comb shape for both its kanban and its window design.

They also make their own statement about the merchants who used them. The generic name for the old-fashioned Japanese merchant was *chōnin*, literally "townsman." In a country now famous for its computerized planning, technological drive and multinational market techniques, the old merchant of Osaka or Tokyo is an almost vanished species. But his business philosophy, his ethics and his energy played a major role in developing Japan's business society of today. Most of the stores and the products symbolized by the kanban in these pages no longer exist. But their tradition, their techniques, their whole business outlook, live on in their modern descendants.

THE ART OF SIGN-MAKING is by no means dead in Japan. For many restaurants and traditional shops and inns, the wooden sign of the house is something of a treasure. Even the very modern corporation businessman would feel unclothed without his company's small badge in his button hole—in itself, like the classic Mitsubishi diamond symbol, a relic of the emblems which appeared on house flags and old-fashioned sign boards since the early Meiji period. But the classic Japanese kanban, the wooden or metal identity plate of a business, like the cloth curtain *noren* with the same house insignia, were often intricate artifacts of both the Tokugawa and Meiji periods, a span of more than two centuries.

To the Japanese chōnin, the kanban was a symbol as important as the military banner or crest had been to his nominal samurai betters. Those preserved here are fitting memorials to the old city merchants. The chōnin put his stamp on his country's culture, as well as its business, just as decisively as the heavily publicized samurai warrior or other classic prototypes like the ageless geisha or the tireless semi-conductor salesman. The kanban he used to designate and decorate his stores and count-inghouses shed an interesting side-light on Japan's economic history as it passed from feudal society to modern state.

The first Japanese retailers were traveling peddlers. These groups of enterprising and—considering the troubled times of the warring middle ages—courageous hustlers trudged the length of Japan's warring provinces, their wares most likely

FIGURE 9. This woodblock print dated 1685 illustrates an Edo period *kushi-ya*. Its comb-shaped kanban is very similar to the sign, designed two hundred years later, in the preceding illustration. See also Plate 53.

carried in packs dangling from a pole, selling from village to village. They tended to come from certain districts, the provinces of Ōmi and Ise notably. Their irreverent nicknames–"Ōmi robbers and Ise beggars"–suggest sharp practices as well as obsequiousness. Some of the successful specialties of these early traveling salesmen were continued well into the present century. The famous Toyama patent medicines, for example, originated when the daimyō of Toyama, cured by a new restorative potion, gratefully gave his local apothecary permission to sell similar medicines throughout Japan. Until the seventeenth century, their methods were crude and haphazard and their sales networks poorly organized, although the Ōmi merchants did show a facility for setting up local branches in the towns they visited.

In the late sixteenth century, Japan's three great military dictators successively fastened their grip on the country; trade was made open and generally safer. Under a stated policy of *raku-ichi raku-za* ("free markets and free guilds") merchants of all kinds were encouraged to trade wherever they could and set up businesses. The old restrictive guilds (*za*) which had developed for centuries in Japan's few urban trading centers were either dissolved or transformed. After Tokugawa Ieyasu finally disposed of his last rival's successor and set up his unitary Shogunate as Japan's national government, merchants were encouraged to settle and establish permanent shops. With no more wars and civil disturbances cut to a minimum, it became both safe and profitable to set up specialty stores, not only in the growing metropolises of Osaka, Kyoto and Edo, but in the castle towns where local daimyō ran their fiefdoms, with the Shogun's permission.

Traveling northward towards Edo (the present Tokyo) with the closely guarded Dutch trading mission from Nagasaki, the German physician Engelbert Kaempfer could write in 1692: "I could not help admiring the number of shops we met within all the cities, towns and villages, whole large streets being scarce anything else but continued rows of shops on both sides and I own, for my part, that I could not well conceive how the whole country is able to furnish customers enough, only to make the proprietors get a livelihood, much less to enrich them."

At the time he wrote Osaka and Edo were among the world's largest cities. Edo's population was approaching one million. Merchants both there and in the ancient capital of Kyoto had

FIGURE 10. The design of the paper-covered folding fan (opposite, left), as a symbol and as an object, has remained unchanged for generations. This sign for a fan shop in contemporary Kyoto is little different from the kanban illustrated in Plate 49, dating from the late Meiji period.

FIGURE 11. The fan shape was frequently adopted for its symbolic connotations of luck, and for its graceful design, by shops selling products other than fans. The fortuitous shape (opposite, right), identifies a souvenir shop in contemporary Kyoto; in Plate 94, the fan shape identifies a kite shop.

FIGURE 12. The lucky graphic shape and the fan itself are displayed in multiples on the facade of a modern Takayama fan shop (opposite, below).

FIGURE 13. This book illustration from the early Edo period shows the fan shape used for both the realistic *mokei kanban* and printed on the cloth *noren*.

FIGURE 14. Oversized wooden clogs are used for display in the front window of a *geta* shop in the Kappabashi section of Tokyo. A similar advertising technique from the Meiji period is illustrated in Plate 44.

of Kyoto had already developed specialty quarters. Not the least reason for the profusion of kanban was the merchants' need to establish the identity and attractiveness of a single store in a quarter devoted to shops selling much the same merchandise. They had to advertise, also, in a way that would entice customers without seeming too showy or blatant. Japan's Tokugawa rulers tended to frown on excess display, particularly during their periodic fits of Puritanism. The shape and size of commercial kanban were often regulated by the Shogun's meticulous bureaucrats.

An equally important reason for a well-designed and artistic kanban was to express the character of the merchant. As the great trading houses developed, their masters infused their noren and kanban with the same symbolic value which the samurai gave to his crest. Many of the great houses of chōnin were, in fact, descended from samurai families. Some had slipped into trade when their houses ended up on the losing side of the sixteenth century civil wars. The Mitsui family, for example, lost its fief after losing a campaign to the forces of Oda Nobunaga. The first Sumitomo were also samurai, as was the house of Mitsubishi, whose founder, Iwasaki Yatarō, started in trade with a government subsidy, after being on the winning side with the Imperial troops in the Meiji Restoration.

I T TOOK CONSIDERABLE SOCIAL COURAGE for a man to abandon samurai status and go into trade. Tokugawa Ieyasu and his successors had revived their own variety of state Confucianism—suitably abridged from the teachings of China's Chu Hsi school—as the theoretical underpinning for stratifying Japanese society. In the classic *shi-nō-kō-shō* system—for "warrior, farmer, artisan and merchant"—the samurai nobility *(shi)* occupied the first place. Government was to be their prerogative, executed through an intricate bureaucracy depending on the Shogunate. The farmers *(nō)* came next. Although subject to constant exactions of the Shogun and the local daimyō overlords, the farmer held, in principle at least, a generally respected position. The whole economy of that time depended on the rice he grew. The artisan *(kō)* was next, prop-

FIGURE 15. This plate from a book printed in 1797 illustrates a kanban for *tabi,* shaped like the pattern from which these socks are cut. This shape has been used consistently to the present day for *tabi* shop signs.

regarded as a useful provider of necessary services. The merchant (*shō*) was spurned as a second-class citizen because he dealt in money and kept profits. Money was a commodity which the true samurai almost ritually avoided touching. As the eighteenth century Tokugawa moralist Kumazawa Banzan wrote: "Money is to be despised by the superior man." An expression popular in that day put the chōnin fastidiously in his place: "The offspring of a toad is a toad; the offspring of a merchant is a merchant."

There were, nonetheless, some far-sighted Japanese who grasped the fact that the end of the warring centuries had put an end to the traditional function of the samurai nobility and paved the way for a different kind of society, however long it might take to emerge. In 1615, Tokugawa Ieyasu captured Osaka castle from the last of his rivals, the great Hideyoshi's son Hideyori, thereby consolidating the authority of the Tokugawa house and the power of the Shogunate. In that same year, Mitsui Sokubei, founder of the great merchant family that bears his name, made the decision to abandon the military life for trade. His reasons, as tradition recorded them, were plain and simple: "A great peace is at hand. The shogun rules firmly at Edo and with justice. No more need we live by the sword. I have observed that great profit can be made honorably. I shall brew sake and soy sauce and we shall prosper."

A generation later Sokubei's third son, Hachirobei, made business history by hanging the famous sign "*Genkin, kakene nashi*" ("cash business only, no double pricing") over the family's dry-goods store in Edo, the Echigoya, which was the direct forerunner of Tokyo's modern Mitsukoshi department store. Although the Mitsui were already in a variety of businesses, from money-lending to Sokubei's original sake brewery, the new store proved a sensation. For the first time a Japanese chōnin had broken with the tradition of haphazard custom selling, as well as the sharp practices of the Omi merchants, and introduced a system of regular mass-market sales with standardized pricing. Service was the Echigoya's watchword. As the novelist and essayist Ihara Saikaku wrote admiringly, "When ceremonial costumes are required in a hurry, the shop lets the servants wait and has the regalia made up immediately by several dozens of their own tailors."

Other merchants followed their example. Imitation flattered the Mitsui business and its famous sign in many ways. Years

FIGURE 16. The dramatic *kanban* (opposite, above) for Fukusuke brand *tabi* is made of painted tin and measures over six feet in diameter. Its aesthetic and its appeal are typical of the Taishō Era in which it was made.

FIGURES 17 AND 18. These photographs of contemporary shops advertising traditional products show a striking contrast in aesthetics. A *sake* brewery in Takayama (left) displays a ball of cedar twigs called a *sakabayashi*. The *sakabayashi* has been used to lure customers to taste the new brew since the Kamakura Period and may be the oldest kind of *kanban*. The shop selling Castella pound cake (right) is a landmark in Nagasaki. This confection has been produced since the 1700s when Spanish sailors from the Dutch trading post on Dejima introduced the recipe to local cuisine.

FIGURE 19. This detail of a Meiji Period woodblock print documents the roof and folding doors which protected elaborate *kanban* from the elements. A similar *kanban* is illustrated in Plate 82.

later a hustling brothel proprietor in the Edo Yoshiwara sent out handbills advertising his ladies' services at "cash only, no double-pricing."

IN THE JAPANESE TRADITION, THE MERCHANTS thought of their business as family enterprises. As the great houses of Osaka developed, like Mitsui, Kōnoike and Yodoya, a ceremonial tradition of hierarchy and custom evolved, in its way as complex as samurai etiquette. Continuing and standardizing the mediaeval tradition, young employees were taken into the merchant house as apprentices (detchi). There they learned by doing, under the guidance of the master and the skilled senior workmen. After some ten years of training, the apprentice, generally aged seventeen or eighteen, could advance to the rank of journeyman (tedai). By this time the young worker had already spent perhaps ten years in a particular merchant house. His schooling, such as it was, was at the work-place. His world was bounded by the house which had taken him in. After years more of training he could become a senior clerk (bantō) and assume a position of some responsibility.

On occasion, a bantō might be adopted into the family of the merchant house or, with certain reservations, be allowed to form a house of his own. But the interests of the senior house (honke) were paramount. Branches of the parent house could be formed, in different localities or to handle different kinds of trade. They generally took their cue from the head of the house and were governed by its house laws.

Merchant houses in turn were organized into guilds (kabunakama) regulated by the Shogunate. The Tokugawa guild covered almost every variety of business–rice warehouses, local manufactures and money-lending–and grew very powerful. As the rice economy of the feudal days turned into a money economy, the once lowly merchant's money began to control feudal lords and samurai, who were generally heavily in his debt. With greater wealth and influence, pride in one's house intensified. Profits were often large. Since the samurai, who did not touch money themselves, were naive in business matters, they found themselves more and more at the mercy of the merchants who possessed the wherewithal to finance their often

FIGURES 20 AND 21. The trademarks (left) were featured on Meiji period signs advertising a variety of products. The trademarks (above) identify famous brands of *sake* (clockwise from top right): Kenbishi, Kamiya no Kiku, Nanatsu Ume, Mitsu Uroko, Saruwaka, Jukai or Kotobuki-zake, Masamune, Yoneki no Yone.

extravagant lifestyles. Rice stipends received from a fief were frequently mortgaged to an Osaka merchant or moneylender for years ahead.

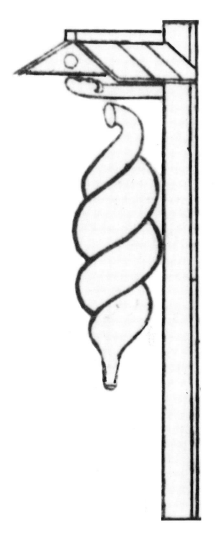

To most merchants, profits were secondary to increasing one's share of the market and thus insuring the growth and permanency of the senior merchant house—an interesting portent of modern Japanese multinational business strategies. In their efforts to enhance the prestige of their particular house and to differentiate it from its competitors in the same guild, the chōnin set ever greater store on signs and symbols. The modest kanban of the early Tokugawa period grew bigger and bigger. The lavishness of their gold, silver and mother-of-pearl ornaments had to be regulated by decrees of the Shogunate, whose Confucian-minded retainers continued to oppose any excess of show on the part of the lower classes.

Where size and expense were restricted, ingenuity took over. Often the signs themselves were puns or figurative allusions to the business of the store concerned. A comb manufacturer in Edo period Kyoto displayed a sign with the letter 13, pronounced *jū-san* in Japanese, since the word for comb *kushi* could be read as 9 *(ku)* plus 4 *(shi)*, making thirteen. His colleagues widely adopted the luckier rendering of thirteen and shops selling combs are still called *jūsan-ya*. A confectionary shop would post a sign with a picture of a wild horse *(ara-uma)* signalizing the words 'ara-umai' – "ah, delicious," by way of stressing the tastiness of the goods. A sake brewer might merely display a bundle of cedar twigs—called a *sakabayashi* (Figure 6)—to display his wares. Sake casks were made of cedar and cedar ashes were used in the brewing process. Dumplings advertised with a picture of a heavy Sumo wrestler, suggested the ample solidity of the food offered for sale at one shop. Sumo wrestlers, geisha and Kabuki actors—all part of the "floating world" popularized in woodblock prints—advertised a wide variety of goods and services.

For the more prominent merchant houses, which had made big businesses out of warehousing, moneylending and commodity speculation or large department stores, the house

Figures 22, 23, and 24. Fish of all sorts and rendered in many mediums are popular symbols for restaurant kanban. The blowfish (opposite, top) identifies a Kyoto restaurant that specializes in this fish delicacy. Painted cement is used for a modern sign on a fish restaurant in the Asakusa section of Tokyo. A huge, red, mechanized crab waves its legs over the entry to a landmark restaurant on Teramachi Street in Kyoto.

Figure 25. A drawing from an Edo period book illustrates a *yane kanban* for a tobacconist's shop. The small roof protected the elaborate pipe carved in the shape of a rolled tobacco leaf.

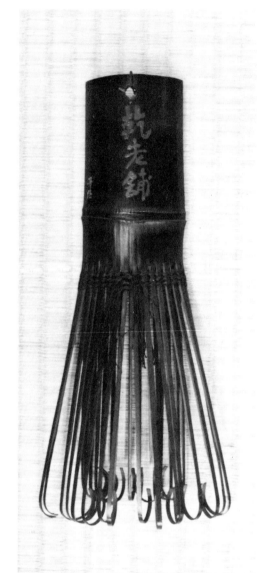

crest on a sign was enough by way of explanation. For modest advertising purposes, it was duplicated on paper lanterns. In Mitsui's successful Edo dry-goods establishment, oiled paper umbrellas with the Mitsui emblem were loaned to customers on rainy days.

T HE USE OF DISTINCTIVE KANBAN AND NOREN, the divided cloth curtain at a store's entrance, found its way into the language. Even today a shopkeeper will announce closing hours with the words *"Kanban desu,"* "It's time to take the sign in." An attractive lady clerk, hired to lure customers to the store, is called a *"kanban musume"* literally "sign-girl." In big businesses as well as small, phrases are still used like *"Noren no ue ni agura o kaku."* Its literal meaning, "Sit down on your trademark," indicates someone who trades on his company's past reputation instead of going out to get more business himself.

Throughout the seventeenth century the power and pelf of the merchants increased. Using their positions as warehouse keepers or purveyors of special goods (*goyō tashi*) to the Shoguns or provincial daimyō, the Osaka merchants and, ultimately, their pushy rivals in Edo, the Shogunate's capital, felt reasonably secure against the anger of their samurai debtors. On occasion, when threats of force were used against them, merchants readily hired gangs of masterless samurai (*rōnin*) as bodyguards for their establishments. In some instances the Shogun authorized confiscation of a merchant house's possessions, as in 1705, when the hugely rich Osaka house of Yodoya was expropriated by the state. And reforming Shoguns like Yoshimune would curb their power by edict. (At one point Shogunate officials ordered all the ornate gilt signs destroyed and restricted kanban to simple black lettering describing only the product and the house name.) Moralists like the great scholar Ogyū Sorai could denounce the merchants' almost total control of the prices which commoners and samurai alike were forced to pay. "Merchants all over the country," he wrote, "grew powerful and formed themselves into groups. The prices of commodities in castle towns and remote provinces were equalized. The daimyō were no match for these millions of or-

FIGURES 26, 27 AND 28. The shape of the product or the container in which it was sold is the oldest design commonly used for kanban. (Opposite, clockwise from left):

This beautifully carved sign from the collection of the Matsumoto Mingeikan advertised the sharpening and setting of the teeth of saws.

An oversized bamboo tea whisk, bisected to lie flush with the facade, still is used to identify a Kyoto shop selling tea ceremony utensils.

Various brands of sake are identified by the characteristic shape of sake casks mounted on this sign in Nagasaki.

FIGURE 29. This illustration, dated 1839, shows a sign similar to Figure 26 hung with a small roof as protection from the weather. Such architectural elements were probably common throughout the Edo and Meiji periods, but many were discarded when signs were collected for aesthetic value not utilized for commercial value.

Figures 30 and 31. Brush shops were common in the Edo and Meiji periods and their kanban were traditionally one of the following types. Identified, like the shop Heian-dō near Kudanshita in Tokyo, by an oversize sculpted wooden brush carved in the round similar to that illustrated in Plate 97. An incised and painted brush (detail, right) was an equally popular design solution, also seen in Plate 98.

ganized traders." The lonely commentator Andō Shōeki cas-
tigated merchants who "with fair words and a plausible
manner...tell deliberate lies, flatter the upper and lower
classes, deceive each other and even their parents and
brothers."

Much of this criticism was exaggerated. Many of the merchant
houses were directed by honorable men, moralists in their own
right, who found comfort in the teaching of popular philos-
ophers like Ishida Baigan that, in fulfilling their mission of
manufacturing and trading in goods, they were doing the just
thing. "Renounce desires and pursue profits whole-heartedly,"
the earlier Zen master Suzuki Shōsan wrote. "But you should
never enjoy profits. You should, on the contrary, work for the
good of others."

Understandably, however, many of the chōnin were unable to
grasp the moral imperative of using their profits for the public
welfare. After all, the profits were theirs to spend. Barred from
higher social status or political power and educated principally
in the practical arts of shrewd calculation and brisk trading,
the city merchants tended to use their gains in the pursuit of
personal pleasure. Parties and entertainments were one sure
way of showing one's rank and status in the merchant world.
Especially in the new metropolis of Edo, the lavish feast and
the pleasureboat outing on the Sumida River, the new cult of
the *rakugo* comedian and the splashy melodrama of kabuki
replaced the austere tea ceremonies, Zen meditations and Nō
plays of the samurai culture.

I N TIME THE BIG SPENDING OF THE CHŌNIN created its own
popular culture, which had its flowering in the famous age of
Genroku, roughly the close of the seventeenth century and the
first four decades of the eighteenth. This flamboyant bourgeois
culture was a civilization of mode and behavior (*kōdō bunka*,
later Japanese critics called it) in which conspicuous consump-
tion became an art in itself.

Nowhere was this pleasure principle more evident than in the
heavy patronage of the lavishly decorated licensed quarters of
the great cities—whether the Yoshiwara in Edo or the older

FIGURE 32. A traditional kanban for a
brush shop is depicted against a fanciful
landscape of Mount Fuji in this Meiji
period print.

FIGURE 33. The distinctive gritty red clay used to make this sign for an established family kiln is identified with the town of Bizen, famous for its pottery.

FIGURE 34. The bow and arrow was sometimes used for its symbolic value, but here it identifies a Kyoto archery shop. Fine wood and skilled carving make this a powerful graphic image.

Shimabara in Kyoto, where even today some of the historic brothels of those days and before are preserved as (architectural) national treasures.

The samurai class was forbidden to frequent the gay quarters. Penalties were visited on those caught there, in accordance with the Shogunate's strict Confucian house rules. Not for the Tokugawa warrior class was the discreet dalliance of an earlier day, which the pages of *Genji Monogatari* have memorialized. But no such restrictions were laid on the merchants. In an odd contrast to Europe, where the fashionable Don Juans and Casanovas were members at least of the minor nobility, the lady-killer of Tokugawa Japan was the friendly local businessman, relaxing after a hard day selling kimono-cloth, face powder, patent medicines or fish. A whole picaresque literature developed to describe the multiple nightly assignations and expensive banquets of the merchants and their etiquette-ridden girl friends, while the wives obediently sat at home. "Japan," wrote the Meiji educator Fukuzawa Yukichi some years later, "is a woman's hell." Ihara Saikaku, a merchant's son himself, wrote classic novels like *The Life of an Amorous Woman* and *The Life of an Amorous Man*, in which he chronicled the after-hours complications of the Edo and Osaka merchants. The mentality of the counting house pervaded even the romantic life of the merchant. One of Saikaku's heroes, Yonosuke, records active sexual relations with exactly 725 women and some varieties of social activity with some 3,000 more. Chikamatsu Monzaemon, often called Japan's Shakespeare, wrote dramas for the *Bunraku* or the Kabuki stage about tragic double suicides *(shinjū)*, where the hapless money merchant and his courtesan lover, finally bankrupt of both ready cash and emotions, did themselves in. One such romance, the famous *Shinjū Ten no Amijima (Double Suicide at Amijima)*, the story of the desperate love of Jihei, the paper-seller and the courtesan Koharu, was transferred to the screen in 1969 by Masahiro Shinoda's brilliant film of the same name.

I NEVITABLY THE CULTURE OF THE TIME reflected the tastes of the merchants for the gaudy and decorative. Its most representative graphic art became the *ukiyo-e* print and its theater

FIGURE 35. This woodblock print shows an Osaka shop where skilled metalworkers crafted decorative hardware for doors and furniture. The kanban illustrated in the print is similar to Plate 39.

FIGURE 36. The popular sumo wrestler, symbol of strength, identified a variety of products (see Plates 10 and 96). Here he advertises a patented treatment for anemia.

FIGURES 37 AND 38. Painted tin signs, easily mass-produced, became popular at the turn of the century. The Meiji fascination with things foreign is evident in these brightly painted signs for tobacco. The panel, left, advertises "Native Brand" cigarettes.

the Kabuki. Not for the chōnin were the subtle poetry-readings of the Ashikaga shoguns' court society or the literary romances of a Prince Genji, where the correct poem after leave-taking was as important to the principals as the love-play which inspired it. The chōnin of Osaka wanted their pleasures fast and in quantity, along with the gold chests, intricately carved netsuke ornaments, rich porcelain and beautifully cut silk or brocade clothing they commissioned. It was during the Edo period that the shape of the classic Japanese clothing–the man's *haori* and the woman's kimono–was finally standardized.

Worldly and confident, the merchants not so secretly mocked the Buddhist or Confucian rituals of their social betters in the Tokugawa hierarchy. Burlesques of the old Japanese classics were popular, like the parody of the *Tale of the Heike* where, as Howard Hibbet tells us, the "heroes have been transferred from the late Heian battlefield to the pleasure-quarter." Mocking the memorable opening lines of the *Heike Monogatari* ("The bell of the Gion temple echoes the impermanence of all things"), an early 18th century epic began: "The bells of the Gion festival echo the impermanence of all guests."

THE SIGNS OF THIS TIME reached a new high in their size and the imaginativeness of their decoration. Whether for medicine, fans, cosmetics, food and drink, a kabuki program or a geisha tea-house, the kanban hanging outside was designed to convey a sense of assurance and opulence to the prospective customer. The very name of the era, "Genroku," became synonymous in the modern Japanese language with sudden prosperity and showy display.

The Meiji Restoration of 1868 put an end to the old order of the Shogunate and began an era of enforced modernization. It was the first really great cultural revolution of the modern era in Japan or anywhere else. As Japan modernized, the old noren and kanban gave way to newspaper advertising, poster balloons, neon lighting and ultimately the TV commercial. The merchants of Edo and Osaka participated but little in the industrial and technological upheavals wrought by the Meiji

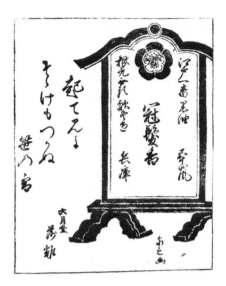

FIGURE 39. A large freestanding sign, termed an *oki kanban*, is depicted in this Meiji period book illustration. When business was still conducted on the tatami mat, these kanban served as space dividers similar to those used today in traditional restaurants. They were also placed in front of a doorway or outside of a shop.

FIGURE 40. This photograph of a street in the Akasaka nightlife district of Tokyo shows the proliferation of contemporary signs, usually rendered in neon.

FIGURE 41. A more traditional, but contemporary, advertisement is this sign for a pickle shop.

reformers. Unlike Europe's bourgeoisie, who helped revolutionize the politics, culture and religion of the Renaissance, the chōnin had been too integral a part of the Tokugawa feudal order to attempt its dissolution; and they rarely aspired to political power. Most of the new big industries set up by the reformers were given to young men of samurai rank to manage. Few of the old merchants kept up with the changes and many went bankrupt in the early Meiji period.

Yet their influence remained as a strong conservative undertow throughout Japanese business. The emphasis on long-term market share over quick profits, the sedulously fostered loyalties of the employee to his house, the imperative to organize competing firms in the same business into trade associations or cartels, the dedication to a craftsman's quality—these marks of the old Osaka chōnin persisted into the Japanese business of today, honored as faithfully as the replicas of kanban and noren which Japanese multinationals use to dignify their product and their house. The presentation of the first kanban used by a Sumitomo on his Edo period pharmacy (Figure 7) remains part of the initiation of employees into that multinational corporation today. The tradition of the Japanese merchant class is thus tangibly preserved.

PLATES

PLATE 1. FUKUSUKE, GOD OF FORTUNE

FOOD AND DRINK

PLATE 2. TEA MERCHANT (detail)

PLATE 2. TEA MERCHANT

34

PLATE 3. MISO SHOP

PLATE 4. SHIROZAKE SHOP

PLATE 5. SAKE BREWER

PLATE 6. SAKABAYASHI   PLATE 7. VINEGAR SHOP

PLATE 8. VINEGAR SHOP

PLATE 9. GREENGROCER

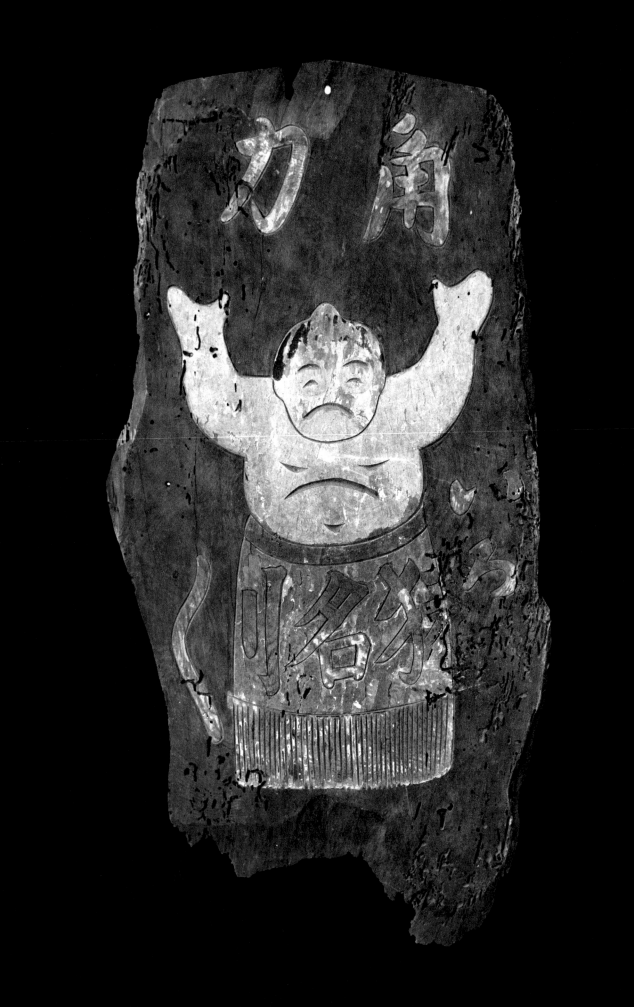

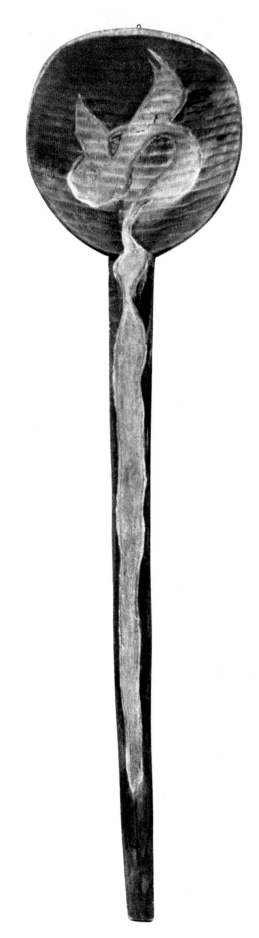

PLATE 10. DUMPLING SHOP   PLATE 11. COFFEE MERCHANT   PLATE 12. FAST FOOD RESTAURANT

PLATES 13 AND 14. TEA SHOP   PLATES 15 AND 16. CANDY SHOP

PLATE 17. TŌFU SHOP   PLATE 18. RICE CRACKER SHOP

PLATE 19. TEA SHOP

PLATE 20. TOBACCO POUCH MAKER   PLATE 21. INRŌ MAKER

PLATE 22. TENGU BRAND TOBACCO SIGNBOARD

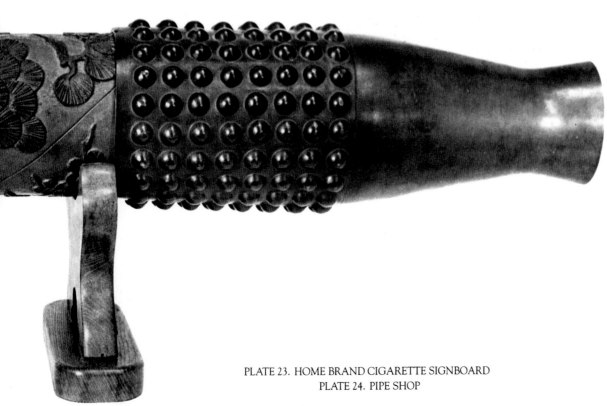

PLATE 23. HOME BRAND CIGARETTE SIGNBOARD
PLATE 24. PIPE SHOP

PLATE 25. TOBACCO SIGNBOARD   PLATE 26. PIPE SHOP

PLATE 27. PIPE AND SMOKING
ACCESSORY SHOP

PLATE 28. BUCKET SHOP

PLATE 29. SAW MAKER

PLATE 30. LOCKSMITH

57

PLATE 31. WATCH REPAIR SHOP

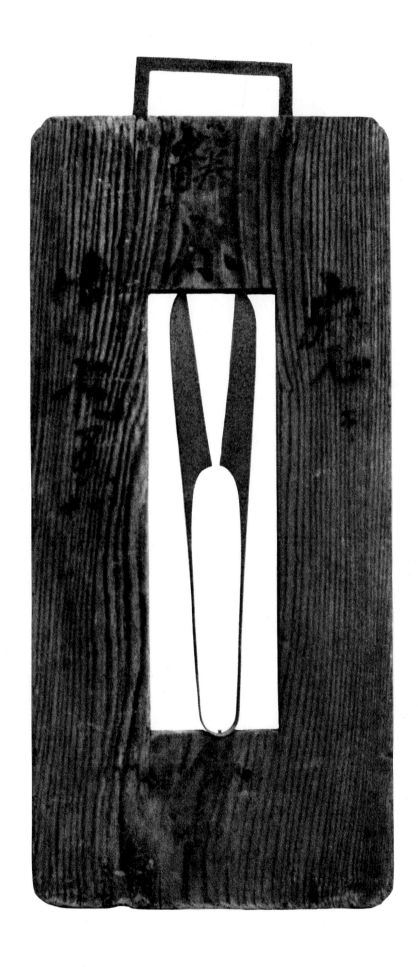

PLATE 32. SCISSOR SHOP

PLATE 33. THREAD SHOP

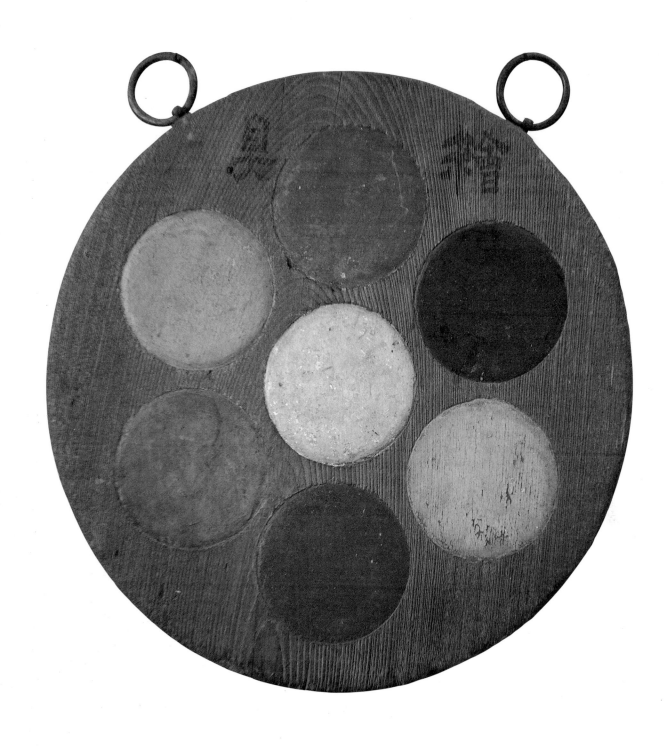

PLATE 34. PAINT SHOP

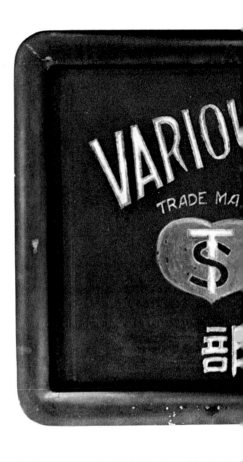

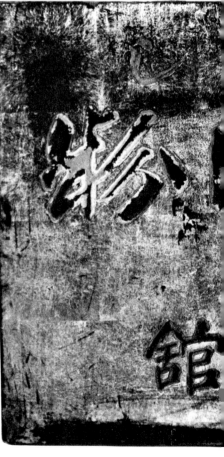

PLATE 35. HAIR CLIPPER SHOP
PLATE 36. SOAP SHOP

PLATE 37. MIRROR SHOP   PLATE 38. TEXTILE DYER AND BLEACHER

PLATE 39. SHOP FOR DOOR PULLS AND HARDWARE

PLATE 40. HARDWARE SHOP

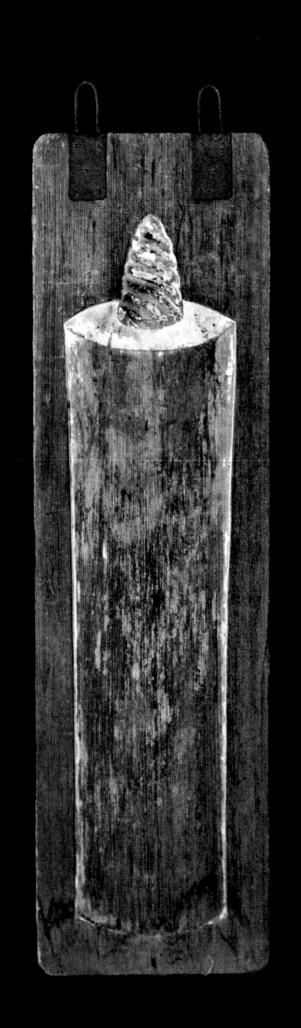

PLATE 41. CANDLE SHOP   PLATE 42. CLOG SHOP

PLATE 43. CLOG MAKER

PLATE 44. CLOG MAKER

(Overleaf)
PLATE 45. TABI SHOP
PLATE 46. SHOE MAKER

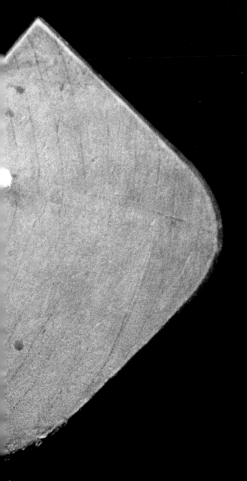

PLATE 47. TEXTILE MERCHANT

PLATE 48. KIMONO SHOP

PLATE 49. FAN SHOP

PLATES 50A AND 50B. WIG MAKER

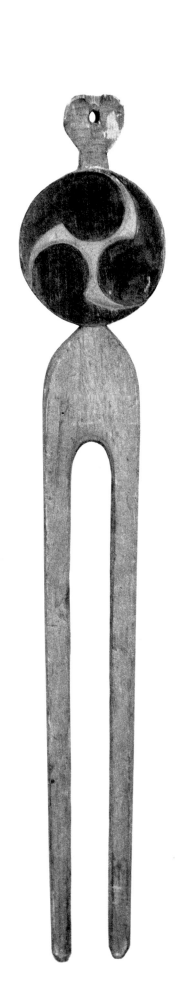

PLATE 51. SHOP FOR HAIR ORNAMENTS   PLATE 52. UMBRELLA SHOP

PLATE 53. COMB SHOP

PLATES 54 AND 55. SHOP FOR
BUDDHIST PRAYER BEADS

PLATE 56. HELMET MAKER

PLATE 57. SCABBARD MAKER

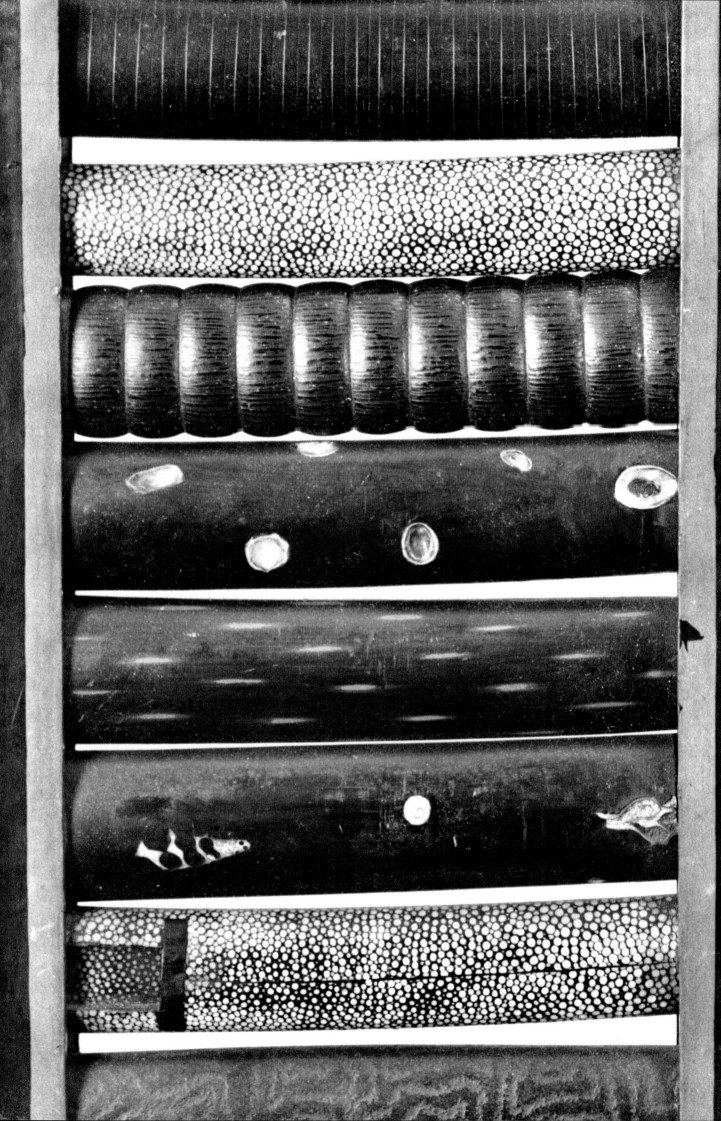

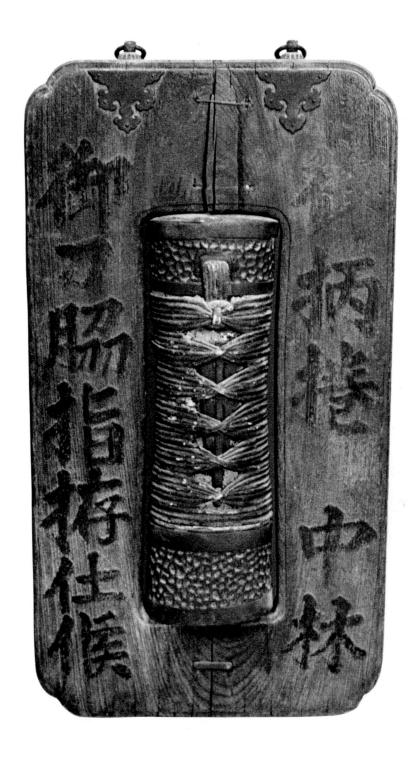

PLATE 57. SCABBARD MAKER (detail)   PLATE 58. SHOP FOR A SWORD HILT WRAPPER

PLATE 59. SCHOOL FOR THE MARTIAL ARTS   PLATE 60. ARROW MAKER

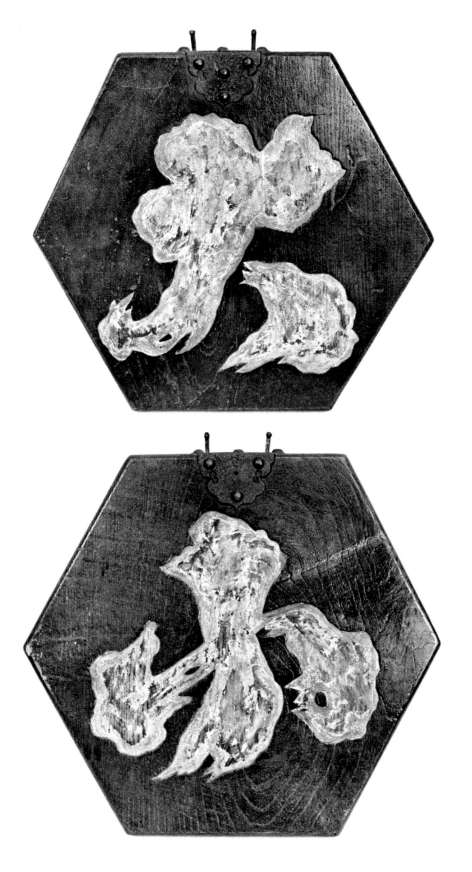

PLATES 61A AND 61B. MONEY LENDER

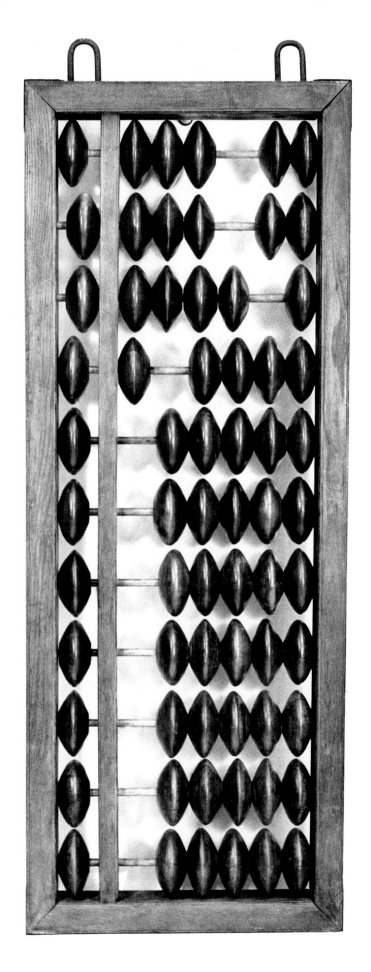

PLATE 62. ABACUS SHOP

PLATE 63. MONEY LENDER
PLATE 64. PAWNSHOP

PLATE 65. COIN EXCHANGE

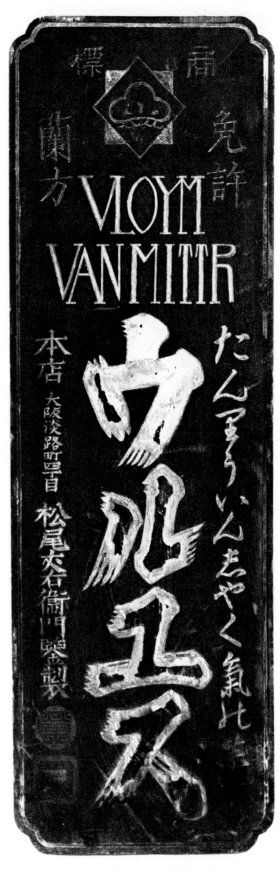

PLATE 66. STATIONERY SHOP   PLATES 67 AND 68. (overleaf) PHARMACY SIGN FOR
                                        "ULUUS" STOMACH MEDICINE

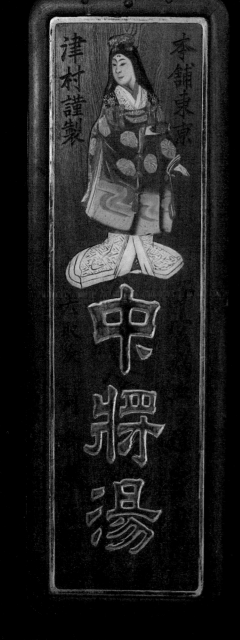

本舗東京
津村謹製
中将湯

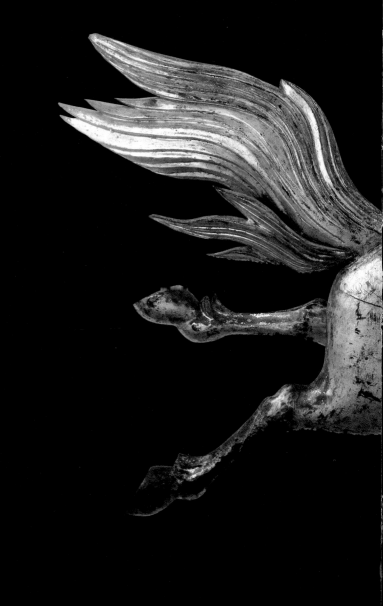

特約 三田村薬舗
プロシン
神薬
薬 一方水 目
本舗 東京資生堂

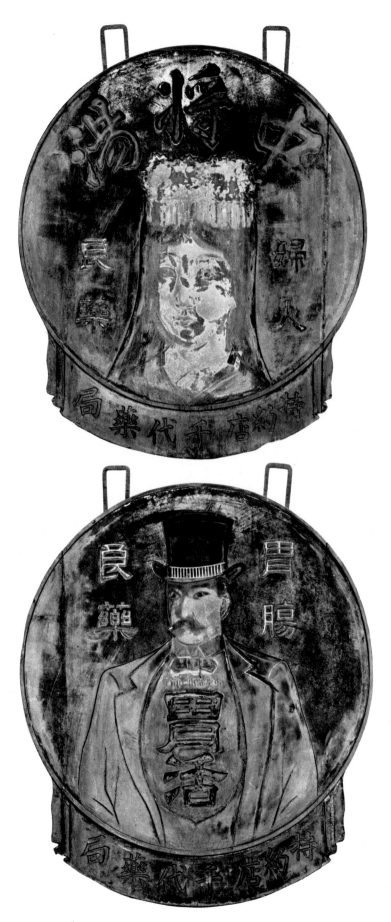

PLATE 69. EYE MEDICINE SIGN
PLATE 70. PHARMACY SIGN FOR
WOMEN'S AILMENTS
(opposite, detail)

PLATES 71A AND 71B. PHARMACY SIGN FOR
"CHŪJŌTŌ" AND "IKATSU" MEDICINES

PLATES 72A AND 72B. PHARMACY SIGN FOR
"HELP" AND "CHŪJŌTŌ" MEDICINES

PLATE 73. PHARMACY SIGN FOR
MENSTRUAL CRAMPS MEDICINE

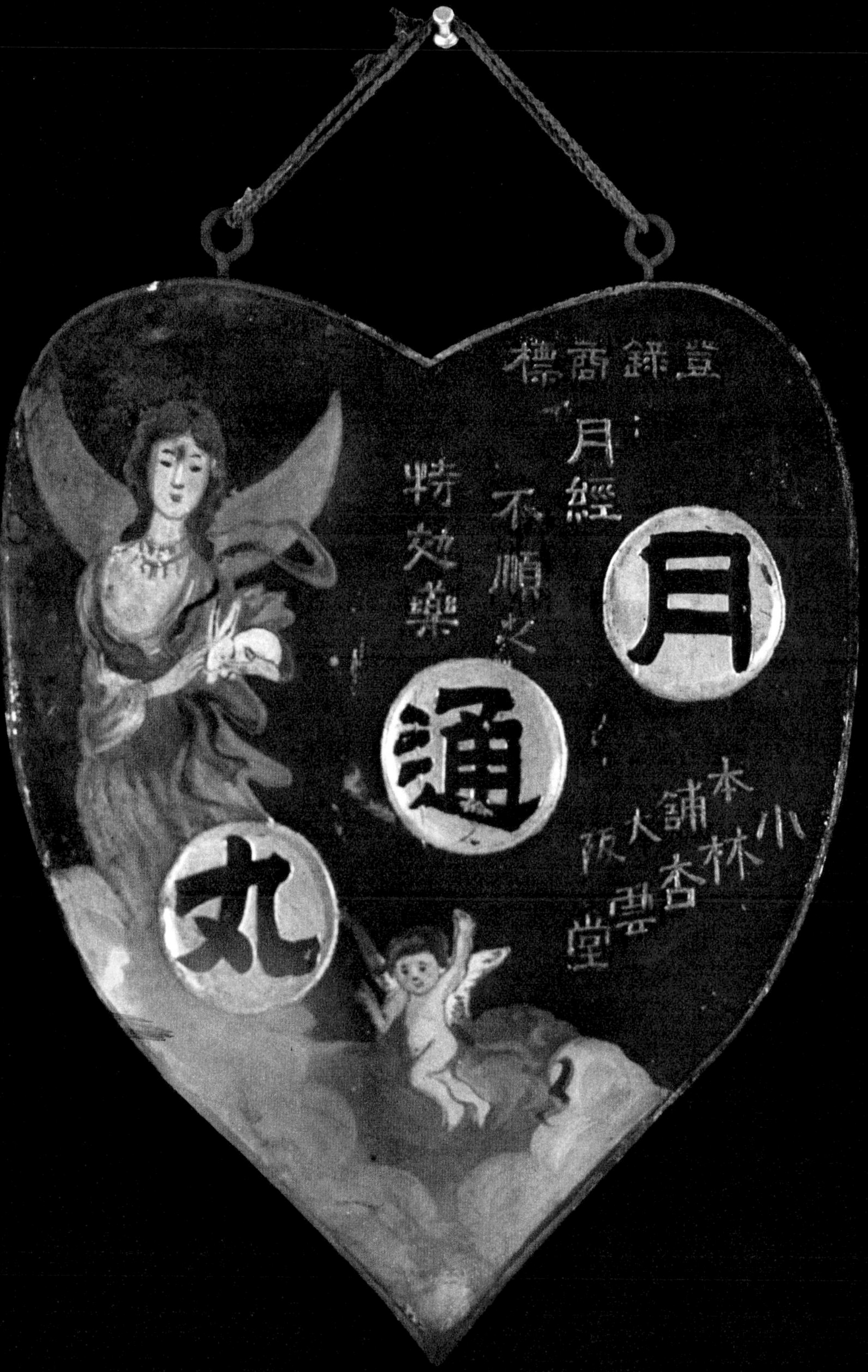
登錄商標
月經不順之特効薬
月通丸
大阪本舗
小林杏雲堂

PLATE 74. PHARMACY SIGN FOR MOTHERS' MEDICINE

PLATE 75. PHARMACY SIGN
FOR A PATENT MEDICINE

PLATE 76. EYEGLASS SHOP

PLATE 77. PHARMACY SIGN FOR EYE MEDICINE PHARMACY

PLATE 78. A PHARMACY SIGN FOR "JINTAN" STOMACH MEDICINE

PLATE 79. PHARMACY SIGN FOR RHEUMATISM REMEDY

PLATE 80. PHARMACY SIGN FOR COLD REMEDY

PLATE 81. PHARMACY SIGN FOR STOMACH REMEDY

PLATE 82. PHARMACY SIGN FOR KIDNEY MEDICINE

PLATE 83. CHIROPRACTOR

PLATE 84. PHARMACY SIGN FOR CHINESE HERBAL MEDICINE

PLATE 85. PHARMACY SIGN FOR PAIN KILLER

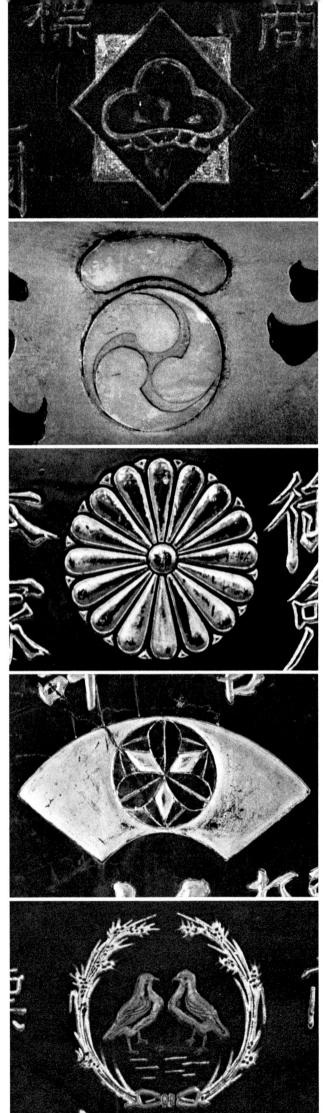

TRADEMARKS FROM PHARMACY SIGNS
PLATE 86. (opposite) PHARMACY SIGN

PLATE 87. INN AT A FERRYBOAT LANDING

PLATE 88. BATHHOUSE

PLATE 89. INCENSE SHOP

PLATE 90. THEATER SIGNS
PLATE 91. TOY SHOP

PLATE 92. TRANSPORTATION SERVICE   PLATE 93. KITE MAKER

PLATE 94. KITE MAKER
PLATE 95. ANTIQUE SHOP

PLATE 96 A AND 96 B. DOLL SHOP OR TEA HOUSE   PLATE 97. BRUSH SHOP

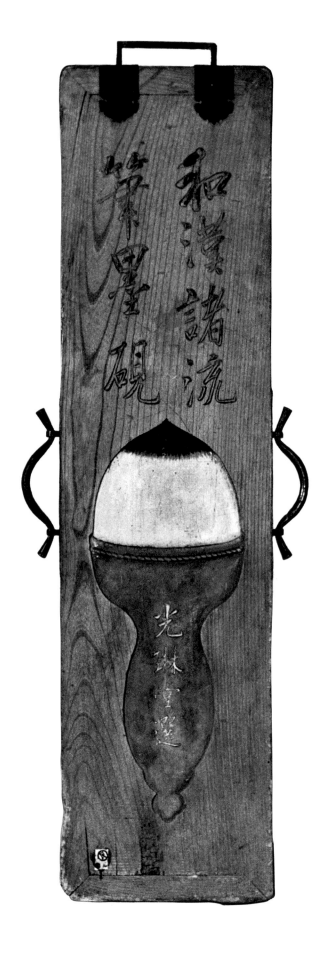

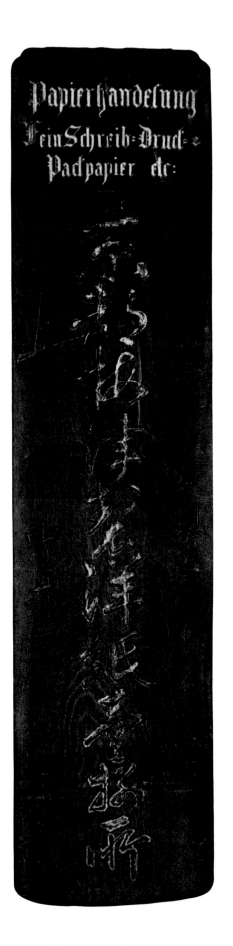

PLATE 98. BRUSH SHOP

PLATE 99. PAPER SHOP

PLATE 100. MUSICAL INSTRUMENTS SHOP

傾國傾城漢武帝
爲雲爲雨楚襄王

PLATE 101. TEA HOUSE IN THE GAY QUARTER

PLATE 102. GEISHA HOUSE

PLATE 103. BOOK LENDER

PLATE 104. KABUKI ACTOR'S SIGN

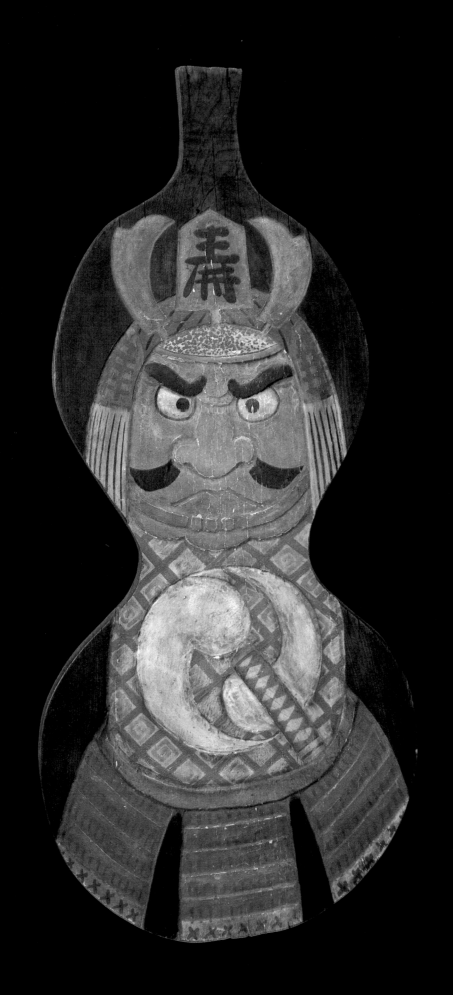

PLATE 105. TOY SHOP   PLATE 106. MANEKI NEKO (BECKONING CAT)

A sign is a formalized means of communication and its essence is language. An understanding of the art of the Japanese written language is, thus, fundamental to the appreciation of kanban. The Japanese imported the Chinese writing system—comprised of ideograms or characters which represent words or concepts and their phonetic renderings—when they adopted other fundamentals of the Chinese civilization during the Asuka and Nara periods (552-794 AD). In emulating and advocating the centralized government, Buddhist faith, ethics, and literature of the continent, the Japanese received the Chinese written language and, in time, adapted it to their own purposes.

There are three principal styles of Chinese calligraphy which the Japanese developed. "Regular script," called *kaisho,* is the standard style which evolved from the squared characters used in the documents and stone inscriptions of the Han dynasty in China. It was intended primarily for official records and *sutra-*writing. "Running script" or *gyōsho* is an abbreviated and slightly looser style of writing than regular script. Its purposes were more informal. The "cursive script" or *sōsho* is the most simplified abstraction of the basic character and necessarily the most expressive. Its elegant fluidity was well-suited to personal correspondence and poetry, and it was practiced and prized on the basis of aesthetics alone.

During the ninth century, the Japanese developed two syllabaries which were combined with the Chinese "one word, one character" ideograms or *kanji.* Based on Chinese characters, each "letter" in the *hiragana* and *katakana* syllabaries represents one sound. The *katakana* is a more squared and angular script, while the *hiragana* is rounded and cursive, like the *sōsho* style.

All styles of *kanji* and the two *kana* syllabaries are used on kanban, although the *sōsho* style was more frequently chosen, because its rounded, running script enhanced the visual beauty of the sign, and because it complemented the *hiragana* which was often incorporated in the writing.

During the Edo period, there was a flowering of calligraphy and a proliferation of design styles used for special purposes: kabuki script for the posters, programs, and costumes of the theatre; woodblock script used in the *ukiyo-e* scenes and book illustrations printed then; sumo script for announcements to the sumo games and all related literature; and there even developed a *kanban-ji,* a script suited to the graphic display and wood-carving of the kanban. Since the basic purpose of kanban is to advertise or communicate information, the use of calligraphy and the choice of its style serves not only to date the piece but must be considered an integral part of the artistic whole.

Various kinds of wood were used for kanban but by far the most common for this purpose was *keyaki* (the zelkova tree), whose durability and good weathering qualities made it particularly suitable. It was also prized for its beautiful grain. Others used were *kiri* (paulownia), a grayish wood with open grain, known to attract worms; *kuri* (chestnut); *sugi* (cryptomeria); and *hinoki* (Japanese cypress) favored for its stability and blond cast.

Many kanban in the entries following could be assigned to more than one descriptive category. For example, a sign hanging under the eaves (*sage* or *nokizuri*) may also be highly decorated (*shōkei*). We have chosen to catalogue each sign below according to its most outstanding characteristic. Most kanban are for kinds of shops, but some are advertisements for brand names, and some are for the maker of a product or for a service rendered.

FUKUSUKE, GOD OF FORTUNE

PLATE 1

37 × 38 cm. (14½ × 15 in.)
Meiji Period
Private Collection
Polychromed wood
MANEKI KANBAN

Irasshaimase, "Welcome to this shop," says Fukusuke, the legendary God of fortune. *Fuku* is a synonym for "wealth" and "happiness," so Fukusuke is truly the merchant's mascot. With his enlarged head and elongated Buddha-ears, he is generally portrayed in a deep bow of greeting.

A popular symbol of good luck, Fukusuke has been mass-produced in inexpensive ceramic and paper-mâché models, but this is a rare prototype of solid wood, carved and lacquered.

TEA MERCHANT

PLATE 2

81.5 × 53 cm. (32 × 21 in.)
Edo Period
Kanichirō Ueda, Kyoto Mingeikan
Polychromed wood
YŌKI KANBAN

Tea leaves in Japan were traditionally stored and packaged in ceramic urns secured with a wooden lid. Hand-blocked rice paper tied with hemp or silk cord sealed the neck of the urn. This kanban is carved in the shape of such an urn and advertises a brand of high-quality tea. The two characters read *Usu-cha,* the more dilute form of thick bitter tea used in the tea ceremony. They are carved in formal calligraphic style and lacquered the green color of the tea. The shop name *Issa-en* appears below. The wrapping of the tea urn is lacquered black and flecked with red, yellow and gold to suggest a decorative paper. The calligraphy which appears over the cord reads *Uji,* a town near Kyoto famous for the cultivation of this kind of tea. Seeds for the tea plant are believed to have been brought from China in the twelfth century by a traveling Japanese Buddhist priest.

MISO SHOP

PLATE 3

75 × 58 cm. (29½ × 23 in.)
Edo Period
Kenichi Higasa Collection, Kobe
Polychromed wood
YŌKI KANBAN

Miso, the soy bean paste which is a staple of the Japanese diet, was an early and common subject of kanban. Miso paste is fermented and stored in large ceramic urns sealed with a wooden lid. Because miso paste was traditionally sold by weight directly from the urns by the owner of the shop, the shape of the container became the common sign of a miso shop.

The rounded, stylized shape of this carving complements the particular design style of the calligraphy, which reads "red and white miso."

PLATE 4.

SHIROZAKE SHOP
34 × 40.2 cm. (13½ × 15¾ in.)
Late Edo/ Early Meiji Period
Peabody Museum of Salem
Polychromed wood
SHŌKEI KANBAN

Shirozake is a thick, sweet drink made from sake and rice malt which is generally served warm in the winter months. The words *kan-jikomi* indicate that the beverage was processed in the winter season.

The kanban for this shirozake shop depicts a famous scene from the *Tales of Ise*, a classic tenth century epic. In this episode, a nobleman and his companions, restless with life in the capital, leave Kyoto to wander the countryside. This scene was later a favorite subject of the Rimpa School of painting and was illustrated by Suzuki Kiitsu (1796-1858) in a painting entitled "Mt. Fuji Episode from the Tales of Ise." Kiitsu depicts the richly dressed nobleman mounted on his horse and attended by his servant, turning to look at Mt. Fuji. This kanban is probably based upon Kiitsu's scene.

This very painterly kanban was probably executed by a professional artist rather than a carver of signs. Gold dust or mica is brushed directly onto the wood and the texture of the grain adds to its beauty. The tasseled silk cord is an additional touch of elegance.

PLATE 5

SAKE BREWER
98 × 87 cm. (38½ × 34¼ in.)
Edo Period
Shōwa Neon Collection, Tokyo
Lacquer on wood
YŌKI KANBAN

Sake has always been an integral part of Japanese life and the number and variety of kanban for it reflect this. Sake is stored in cedar barrels, wrapped in straw. The *shimenawa*, a braided straw rope sacred in Shinto belief and a portent of good luck, was an essential part of the barrel. Often sake kanban too had rope embedded in them. The larger brewers licensed retail shops to display their kanban, like the promotional product advertising still seen in shops. Carved in red, black and gleaming gold lacquer, this kanban for Fukumusume sake is particularly elegant.

Fukumusume sake is a brand that originated in Edo and is still sold today. The kanji at the top, *shōhyō yūken* is terminology used before the Meiji era to signify the right to use a trademark. Various *hanko*, seals, indicate prizes won by this sake.

PLATE 6

SAKABAYASHI
Diameter 66 cm. (30 in.)
Contemporary Period
Private Collection
Cedar twigs
MOKEI KANBAN

Another type of sign related to sake brewing is the *sakabayashi*. Sakabayashi are known to have existed in the twelfth century, making them one of the earliest, if not the earliest, form of kanban. They are large balls of cedar twigs left over from making the cedar sake casks. The hanging of new sakabayashi in the spring of the year indicated that the new sake was ready to drink. One can still observe this custom in Takayama, a town famous for sake-making.

VINEGAR SHOP

PLATE 7

75 × 58 cm. (29½ × 23 in.)
Edo Period
Kanichirō Ueda, Kyoto Mingeikan
Keyaki root
Yōki kanban

In Japan, vinegar—made from rice—is fermented and stored in wooden containers, such as the one suggested by this sign. Made from the burled root of the *keyaki* tree, this sign has a natural surface interest and is more than three hundred years old.

This kanban, which once graced a shop in Nara, was originally in the Sugiura Collection—probably the largest and most well-known collection of signboards ever assembled. Saburobei Sugiura began gathering old Kyoto kanban in 1899 and by the time he died, just before World War II, he had found many hundreds. A fire destroyed much of this collection but fortunately some signs, like this one for vinegar, were saved.

VINEGAR SHOP

PLATE 8

23 × 27 cm. (9 × 10¾ in.)
Edo Period
The Hosoda Collection, Tokyo
Wood
Yōki kanban

The line of the large central *hiragana* character *su* echoed in the contours of this kanban makes an elegant, simple, strong graphic statement. The smaller *kanji* at the top read *gokujōhin*, "top quality."

GREENGROCER

PLATE 9

42 × 91 cm. (16½ × 36 in.)
Late Edo/Early Meiji Period
Peabody Museum of Salem
Polychromed wood
Mokei kanban

This kanban needs little explanation because its graphic statement is simple and eloquent. Depicted in this lively carving is the *daikon*, a kind of radish, fundamental to Japanese cuisine. This sign for a greengrocer is intricately carved and was once decorated with color, only faint traces of which remain.

DUMPLING SHOP

PLATE 10

81 × 41 cm. (32 × 16 in.)
Meiji Period
Peabody Museum of Salem
Polychromed wood
Sage kanban

The figure of the sumo wrestler with its implications of supernatural strength and health was frequently used on signs for medicines and food. The wrestler Inagawa, whose name appears on the apron, was a popular hero. Born in 1871 in Gumma-ken, he won the championship in the tournament of January 1900 with a record of 8-1. This kanban was probably made shortly after that time, since Inagawa was then famous enough to be used for promotional purposes.

This painted kanban advertises *manjū*, dumplings made of sweet red or white bean paste. It is made of *kiri*, paulownia wood.

PLATE 11

COFFEE MERCHANT
76 × 30 cm. (30 × 12 in.)
Meiji Period
Kenichi Higasa Collection, Kobe
Lacquered wood
SAGE KANBAN

Foreign words from Western languages were introduced into Japanese advertising during the Meiji era and imparted a sense of excitement, identifying the product as both new and imported. *Dai Nihon Saisho,* "first in Japan," proclaims this sign for "Kōhītō," a new brand of coffee with sugar. Four different typographic styles are combined on this single panel.

PLATE 12

FAST FOOD RESTAURANT
104 × 25 cm. (41 × 10 in.)
Late Edo/Early Meiji Period
The Hosoda Collection, Tokyo
Polychromed wood
MOKEI KANBAN

The sign of the long spoon advertised a restaurant whose specialty was simple rice dishes. *Meshi* is a generic term for both "boiled rice" and "meal." Eating places, known as *ichizen meshiya* (*ichizen* for "one bowl of rice") were cheap and common. The two *hiragana* characters spelling *Meshi* have been written in an exaggerated way to follow the contours of the kanban.

PLATE 13

TEA SHOP
95 × 61 cm. (37½ × 24 in.)
Edo Period
Shōwa Neon Collection, Tokyo
Polychromed wood
SAGE KANBAN

This kanban was chosen for its historical interest rather than its aesthetics. It announces that a tea shop, Yamashiro, near Kyoto, was awarded a first prize, *ittō-shō,* for its tea leaves. When this kanban was carved, the use of the Imperial crest with its sixteen-petalled chrysanthemum was permitted. With the Meiji restoration of political power to the Emperor, however, it was decreed that only the Imperial Household could use the sixteen-petalled chrysanthemum. The shop owner, too frugal to discard a perfectly good kanban, merely altered the crest so that the chrysanthemum had fewer petals.

PLATE 14.

TEA SHOP
66.1 × 63 cm. (26 × 24¾ in.)
Meiji Period
Peabody Museum of Salem
Lacquered wood
YŌKI KANBAN

The stylized sculpture of the container gives this kanban for a tea shop a special elegance. The use of gold lacquer and the lines of the vessel convey the sense of a high quality product. The calligraphy, in a flowing style which follows the contours of the urn, says *cha,* tea.

CANDY SHOP

PLATE 15

50 × 37 cm. (19¾ × 14½ in.)
Edo Period
Minezō Tani, Tokyo
Polychromed wood
SHŌKEI KANBAN

This elegant sign decorated in gold and red lacquer identified a shop selling *ame*, a generic term for sugar candy. The candy jar is placed on a little dais and the curving style of the calligraphy follows the contour of the vessel. The exposed wood grain adds textural contrast.

The writing at the bottom reads *Kōkō* (the brand of ame), *tō-ya* (sugar shop). On the back is written: *Jiyō oya-dama*, "most nutritious candy."

CANDY SHOP

PLATE 16

44 × 45 cm. (17¼ × 17¾ in.)
Meiji Period
Kenichi Higasa Collection, Kobe
Polychromed wood
SHŌKEI KANBAN

The *tanuki* or badger is credited with magical and supernatural powers. In appearance he resembles a raccoon-faced dog and in the many folk tales told of his exploits he is depicted as mischievous and pleasure-loving. He is said to appear on rainy moonless nights disguised as a mendicant Buddhist priest and exhibits an inordinate capacity for sake. He is frequently portrayed in a priest's hat, a straw raincoat bulging over a belly full of sake, with a wine bottle slung over his shoulder. He is often placed before shops as a figure of welcome. This tanuki lured customers to buy *o-kashi*, sweets, advertised on his belly.

TŌFU SHOP

PLATE 17

128 × 40 cm. (50½ × 15¾ in.)
Late Edo Period
The Hosoda Collection, Tokyo
Wood
YAKATA KANBAN

This sign for a *tōfu*, soy bean curd, shop is characteristic of *yakata* kanban, the most architectural classification of signboards. It was designed to fit into a door frame. The cursive calligraphy carved against the grain of the *keyaki* wood is legible from either direction. The text is rendered in *kanji* on one side and in *hiragana* on the other. The hiragana side adds the word for happiness implying that "Tōfu makes you happy." The kanji, *meibutsu*, in the upper corner of both sides means "local specialty."

RICE CRACKER SHOP

PLATE 18

44 × 45 cm. (17¼ × 17¾ in.)
Edo Period
Kenichi Higasa Collection, Kobe
Polychromed wood
SHŌKEI KANBAN

This kanban is realistically carved in the form of a shell. Its imagery is borrowed from the folk tales of the heroic general, Benkei, whose great strength and prowess helped the Genji clan defeat the Heike clan in the twelfth century wars. Benkei, who was immortalized in the classic *Tales of Heike*, became an itinerant Buddhist priest, and is often represented with a conch shell horn, an attribute of the *yamabushi* (wandering priests). Since Benkei was also known for his rather boisterous nature, he was sometimes depicted inside a huge conch shell drinking sake to his heart's content. This legend indicates the proverbial sense of the phrase *horafuki*, blowing the conch, which means "to boast." With the shell as his symbol, this merchant needed only inscribe the product being sold, *sembei*, and this sign boasted for its owners.

PLATE 19

TEA SHOP

38.7 × 88.6 cm. (15½ × 35 in.)
Meiji Period
Peabody Museum of Salem
Polychromed wood
SHŌKEI KANBAN

This kanban is striking for its carving of the silhouette of Mount Fuji traversed by layers of mist. The surface has been left unpainted so that the grain of the *keyaki* wood becomes a dramatic element. The three characters read *cha no kuni ichi,* "best tea in the country." They are carved and painted in pigment. The seal carved on the left is possibly that of the shop owner. Mt. Fuji is located in Shizuoka, the prefecture where the finest tea is grown. The shape of the sign thus suggests the origin of the product.

TOBACCO AND RELATED OBJECTS

The number of signs for tobacco, pipes and the accoutrements of smoking is exceeded only by those for medical products and services. Tobacco was introduced to Japan by European traders in the 16th century and was outlawed for sanitary reasons in 1609, but the edict proved difficult to enforce and was repealed in 1716. The government hoped that the tobacco crop would be beneficial to the economy and, in 1904, it made the tobacco industry a government monopoly, reserving all profits for itself.

Smoking became popular with both aristocratic and merchant classes, although the etiquette of the smoking ritual was different for each class. Traditionally, samurai and aristocrats did not carry tobacco and pipes, but they did wear the case for medicinal herbs *(inrō)*. It was acceptable for commoners, particularly wealthy merchants, to wear the smoker's ensemble—a pipe case *(kiseruzutsu)* and tobacco pouch *(tabako-ire)* or tobacco case *(tonkotsu)* lashed with a cord regulated by a sliding bead *(ojime)*.

Wealthy merchants and Kabuki actors set the fashion in smoking accessories and created a lively demand for the shops that sold and the craftsmen who produced these elegant objects. The finest ivory, metal and lacquer craftsmanship was required and many pipe case artisans, like netsuke-carvers, signed their pieces. The elegant and lavish materials used for the objects are often copied in the kanban design. A good example is the red leather pouch from the Kenichi Higasa Collection (Plate 20).

PLATE 20

TOBACCO POUCH MAKER

35 × 30 cm. (14 × 12 in.)
Meiji Period
Kenichi Higasa Collection, Kobe
Leather, brass, metal
JITSUBUTSU KANBAN

During the Meiji period, pipe accessories—pouches and pipe cases—became particularly elaborate. This red leather pouch with brass and silver fittings is a particularly fine example. The pouch is connected by intricate metal chains to a round metal disk which serves the function of a netsuke.

The pipe case is always used with a tobacco pouch, and assembled in the manner depicted on this sign.

INRŌ MAKER

PLATE 21

112 × 16.5 cm. (44 × 6½ in.)
Late Edo Period
Kenichi Higasa Collection, Kobe
Polychromed wood, silk
JITSUBUTSU KANBAN

The hereditary craft of lacquer found new avenues of expression in the seventeenth and eighteenth centuries when *inrō* (literally, "seal case") became necessary to a proper gentleman's attire. Seal cases hung by a silk cord secured to the *obi* (sash) by a netsuke (toggle). These tiered boxes were used originally to hold chops (seals) but were later adapted to carry medicinal herbs–including myrrh, dragon's blood, musk, cinnamon and ginseng–rather than tobacco. Because seal cases were one of the luxury items not subjected to sumptuary laws, wealthy samurai and the rising merchant class commissioned lacquer artists to create elaborate pieces. The kanban for *inrō*-makers received the same care and attention as the objects themselves. This oversized model of an inrō in black lacquer with silk tassels and a family crest is a good example.

TENGU BRAND TOBACCO SIGNBOARD

PLATE 22

51 × 103 cm. (20 × 41 in.)
Meiji Period
Shōwa Neon Collection, Tokyo
Polychromed wood
NIKAI KANBAN

This sign for Tengu Tobacco was found throughout Japan in the first half of the Meiji era and today is found frequently in collections, including that of the Tobacco and Salt Museum. The founder of Iwaya Tengu Shōkai, producers of Tengu Tobacco, was a colorful character whose tale was told often by the *kōdan-shi*, story-tellers. He always wore a kimono woven with a repeat pattern of the Satsuma crest–a red cross within a circle–although he was not a member of the clan.

The Satsuma family grew more tobacco on their lands in southern Kyūshū than any other producer of tobacco in the Meiji era. Iwaya bought his tobacco from Satsuma and marketed it under various names. The lower portion of this kanban lists several types–Army Tengu, Navy Tengu, Eagle and Red. Iwaya used the distinctive Satsuma crest on his kanban as well as his person.

The Tobacco Monopoly Law making it illegal for private companies to produce tobacco, was passed on April 10, 1904. This kanban could not have been used after that date.

HOME BRAND CIGARETTE SIGNBOARD

PLATE 23

76 × 39 cm. (30 × 15½ in.)
Meiji Period
Tobacco and Salt Museum, Tokyo
Painted tin
SHŌKEI KANBAN

Tin signs became prevalent during the Taishō era (1912-1926) but this one pre-dates 1904 when the tobacco industry was made a government monopoly. The private enterprise of Murai Bros. and Co., Kyoto manufacturers of Home Cigarettes, would have been outlawed by the Tobacco Monopoly Proclamation. The Murai Bros. sign has all the hallmarks of a modern company in Meiji terms–the Western style, abbreviated name rather than the Japanese-style, the use of English on both the sign and the package. The diamond-shaped M in the winking eye is a clever and memorable trademark.

PLATE 24

PIPE SHOP
Length 124 cm. (49 in.)
Meiji Period
Peabody Museum of Salem
Wood and metal
Mozō KANBAN

This oversized pipe is a striking model of a traditional *kiseru*, Japanese pipe. Its metal bowl and mouthpiece are attached by a wooden tube carved with alternating spirals of bamboo leaves and cherry blossoms.

PLATE 25

TOBACCO SIGNBOARD
94 × 61 cm. (37 × 24 in.)
Meiji Period
Heineken Family Collection, Princeton, N.J.
Wood, paper and lacquer
MOKEI KANBAN

The *daruma*, a popular symbol of good fortune in Japan, appears frequently on kanban advertising a variety of products. Here the daruma identifies a brand of tobacco. This kanban originally hung from a shop in Kagoshima, southern Kyūshū. Rope burns indicate that the sign was anchored at right angles to the building to prevent it from swinging. The *sugi* wood was deeply carved in an intricate tobacco leaf pattern and covered with successive layers of mulberry paper, a sealer made from powdered clam shells, and lacquer. His protruding glass eye gives this daruma a wonderfully fierce look.

PLATE 26

PIPE SHOP
81.5 × 24 cm. (32 × 9½ in.)
Late Edo/Early Meiji Period
Tobacco and Salt Museum, Tokyo
Brass and wood
MOKEI KANBAN

Sumptuary laws intended by the daimyo to keep the merchant class in its place were indeed the "three day laws" that they were popularly called. The prohibition of gold lacquer and other lavish excesses on kanban did not halt production of elegant signs like this for a pipe shop. The stem of the pipe is shaped like a rolled tobacco leaf and is made of brass.

PLATE 27

PIPE AND SMOKING ACCESSORY SHOP
125 × 41 cm. (49 × 16 in.)
Late Edo Period
Japan Folk Crafts Museum, Tokyo
Polychromed wood and copper
SAGE KANBAN

Not all pipe shop signs seduced the eye with gold lacquer and extravagant materials. This one of metal and wood had a rustic quality typical of many Edo kanban. The technique of insetting metal into wood was a special skill of the kanban maker and here the copper is cleverly contrasted with the grain of the wooden shank. The pouch and pipe case above is carved and painted. The calligraphy beside the stem seems almost to be a careless addition. It says *oroshi* ("wholesale") and *ko-uri* ("retail").

BUCKET SHOP

PLATE 28

38 × 43 cm. (15 × 17 in.)
Meiji Period
Kenichi Higasa Collection, Kobe
Polychromed wood, wire
MOKEI KANBAN

Three interlocking circles make a handsome graphic symbol for a bucket shop. Wire banding, such as would be used to fix a real bucket, adds a realistic touch to this kanban. The inscription is colorful–both literally and figuratively. The character in the right circle is *dai* (alternately, *tai*), "large"; the one on the left is *fū*, "wind." The compound *taifū* is commonly used for hurricane, gale or high wind, although the proper Japanese character reading for typhoon uses a different first character for *tai.* The top circle bears the symbol for a standard measure called a *masu*. The character *masu*, which does not appear on the sign, means "to increase." This implies that the "great wind" brought fires and, thus, prosperity to the bucket merchant. This sign is a good example of the visual puns that were so essential to the Japanese kanban tradition.

SAW MAKER

PLATE 29

136 × 45 cm. (53½ × 17¾ in.)
Edo Period
Kenichi Higasa Collection, Kobe
Wood, *sumi* ink, lacquer
MOKEI KANBAN

Metal craftsmen in the Edo period were highly specialized: scissors, door handles or pulls, nuts and bolts, tools were purchased in separate shops. This sign for a saw maker utilizes the deep grain of the *keyaki* wood to create a strong image. The character, top, reads "guaranteed" and, below, "we buy and sell."

The jagged-toothed saw is lacquered in black on one side. The reverse is painted in *sumi* ink, probably a restoration.

LOCKSMITH

PLATE 30

65 × 45 cm. (25½ × 17¾ in.)
Edo Period
The Hosoda Collection, Tokyo
Wood, iron
JITSUBUTSU KANBAN

This skill of the craftsman is evident in this sturdy signboard for a lock-maker. The heavy iron lock is inset in the *hinoki* board and secured from behind with wooden nails. The shop name, Sanoya, is on the left, and *jōmae* (locks), *hikite rui* (door pulls), and *migaki* (knife sharpening), and other services rendered are listed.

WATCH REPAIR SHOP

PLATE 31

Diameter 60 cm. (23½ in.)
Taishō Period
Museum of Ishikawa Prefecture, Kanazawa
Polychromed wood, metal
MOZŌ KANBAN

Victorian styles strongly influenced Japanese taste in the Meiji period and Taishō era. This colorful dummy of a stop watch is clearly in that tradition. It was the kanban for a watch repair shop outside of Kanazawa. The *kanji* on the face says *shūri*, repair.

PLATE 32

SCISSOR SHOP
73 × 35 cm. (28¾ × 14 in.)
Edo Period
The Hosoda Collection, Tokyo
Wood, iron
JITSUBUTSU KANBAN

In the Edo period, a *hasami-ya* made and sold scissors exclusively. The central pair of real old-style scissors–sharpened blades connected by a flexible iron band–identify this as a *jitsubutsu* kanban. The graceful silhouette of the scissors is placed within the heavily grained *keyaki* wood board, on which the calligraphy is almost too faded to read. The faint words for grinding and sharpening, *migaki,* and the shop name, Fujiwara, are legible.

PLATE 33

THREAD SHOP
33 × 30 cm. (13 × 11¾ in.)
Edo Period
The Hosoda Collection, Tokyo
Polychromed wood
MOKEI KANBAN

Certain kanban designs identified a product or shop with such clarity and simplicity that they were adopted spontaneously by merchants throughout the country. This effective graphic symbol was used almost universally by thread shops in the Edo period. The thickly lacquered bands of bright color wrapped around two vertical posts represent various colors of thread wound around a bobbin.

PLATE 34

PAINT SHOP
Diameter 37.5 cm. (14¾ in.)
Meiji Period
Peabody Museum of Salem
Polychromed wood
MOKEI KANBAN

The simulated pallette with inset circles of bright color in a *keyaki* disk is a most explicit signboard for a paint shop. In the Meiji period, pigments rather than prepared paints were sold in such an establishment. Pigments derived from both minerals and plants were mixed to order for use in cosmetics, dyes and pottery glazes. The calligraphy reads *enogu,* paint, and the sign is identical on both sides.

PLATE 35

HAIR CLIPPER SHOP
75 × 146 cm. (29½ × 57½ in.)
Meiji Period
Kenichi Higasa Collection, Kobe
Polychromed wood
NIKAI KANBAN

The use of English and the graphic illustration of hair clippers on this amusing kanban demonstrates the Japanese Victorian style and the Meiji psychology of sales. This "foreign" product was actually made in Japan and the sign addresses the Meiji preference for imported goods. The registered trademark, *Asahi tonbo,* combines the rising sun *(asahi)* and the dragonfly *(tonbo).* "Various hair clipper manufactory" was a typical Meiji usage.

SOAP SHOP

PLATE 36

45 × 91 cm. (18 × 36 in.)
Meiji Period
Takayama City Kyōdokan
Polychromed wood
SHŌKEI KANBAN

Kane-oke, a soap shop in Takayama, advertised its specialty brand in a purposely elegant manner. The application of gold leaf and the florid style of calligraphy were intended to appeal to an elite and more affluent public. Red lettering across the top proclaims the soap a "high class dirt remover," *kōtō aka-otoshi*, and the brand name of the powder, "Ofuku Araiko," is written in bolder black lettering.

MIRROR SHOP

PLATE 37

75 × 44.5 cm. (29 × 18 in.)
Edo Period
Peabody Museum of Salem
Polychromed wood
MOZŌ KANBAN

The first mirrors used in Japan came originally from China and Korea in the eighth century. They were typically round, bronze, or polished metal disks with a decorated back and polished front. Some were as big as fifty centimeters in diameter and some were as small as coins. In the late sixteenth century, the Portuguese brought European style mirrors—with handles and reflecting glass—as gifts for the samurai. In the Edo period many types of mirrors were sold and their use documented in *ukiyo-e* woodblock prints and Meiji photographs.

This Edo period kanban, which looks metallic from a distance, is skillfully painted on wood in pastel colors, using two classic decorative motifs—one floral, one with phoenix and clouds.

TEXTILE DYER AND BLEACHER

PLATE 38

115.7 × 59 cm. (45½ × 23 in.)
Edo Period
Peabody Museum of Salem
Wood, metal
MOKEI KANBAN

Like an abstract sculpture, this kanban consists of a thinly sliced piece of wood cut with the grain and shaped to resemble cloth hung to dry. It is a sign for a dyer and bleacher of cotton cloth—an unusual occupation that was much in demand in the early Edo period. These dyers worked with a type of soft material called *sarashi* and came to be known by that name. Sarashi is inscribed on this sign in a flowing *hiragana* script so faint that it is barely legible. The bottom edge of the dripping cloth is so thin that, over the years, the wood has split. This kanban has survived to the present day due to its sturdy frame.

SHOP FOR DOOR PULLS AND HARDWARE

PLATE 39

79 × 37 cm. (31 × 13½ in.)
Edo Period
Japan Folk Crafts Museum, Tokyo
Wood, metal
JITSUBUTSU KANBAN

The fine craftsmanship of this sign advertised the quality of workmanship one could expect at this shop. Actual brass door pulls, nail head covers, and other accessories for sliding doors (*fusuma*) and their architectural framework are inset on this hardwood sign. Samples of various decorative shapes—flowers, leaves, even rabbits—are included. There is no calligraphy on this kanban which uses the objects themselves to convey its message.

PLATE 40

HARDWARE SHOP
150 × 34 cm. (60 × 13½ in.)
Edo Period
Japan Folk Crafts Museum, Tokyo
Wood, wrought iron
JITSUBUTSU KANBAN

Samples of a simpler style of door hardware are exhibited on this late Edo period sign for a Tokyo shop. Calligraphy advertising "assorted metal work for furniture" and "metal work for buildings" was lightly carved and painted on the lower half of both sides of the sign, but much of the paint has washed away. Different objects are inset on either side and the black wrought iron contrasts strikingly with the light grayish tone of the wood.

PLATE 41

CANDLE SHOP
93 × 26 cm. (36½ × 10¼ in.)
Edo Period
Japan Folk Crafts Museum, Tokyo
Polychromed wood
SAGE KANBAN

Regulations governing commercial fairs in the Heian period (794-1185) required a merchant to identify the products for sale with a signboard. In these laws, the *Engishiki,* a prototype of the word kanban is used. Literally it means, "This store sells what you see on this sign." This sign for a candle shop meets the requirements of the *Engishiki* and is one of the earliest types of signs. It once had some calligraphy which years of wind and weather have washed away.

CLOTHING AND ACCESSORIES

PLATE 42

CLOG SHOP
28.5 × 26.6 cm. (11¼ × 10½ in.)
Meiji Period
Peabody Museum of Salem
Wood and cloth
MOKEI KANBAN

The fat cheeks and homely face of Okame-san were a common symbol on *maneki* kanban. Like most maneki symbols, Okame had special appeal to the working classes, to whom this kanban for *geta* (clogs) was addressed. According to Japanese beliefs, the antic Okame restored light to the world by luring the sulking Sun Goddess, Amaterasu Ōmikami, from her cave. The Goddess of Mirth, with overtones of bawdiness, Okame was a popular figure and subject to humorous treatment. This humorous kanban expands the usually rectangular geta shape to accommodate Okame's features and cleverly uses the cloth thongs to simulate her hair line.

PLATE 43

CLOG MAKER
65 × 35 cm. (25½ × 14 in.)
Edo Period
Kanichirō Ueda, Kyoto Mingeikan
Wood and iron
SAGE KANBAN

Geta are the raised wooden clogs traditionally worn with *tabi* (Japanese socks) to protect both women and men from the muddy streets. They are always left outside the door. In early Edo, the kanban for geta often used iron, not wood, clogs and this oversize pair swinging from a pierced board was typical of those seen in the Kyoto area at that time. This sign is direct in communication and rustic in feeling and reflects the fact that geta makers were then considered a very low social caste. The maker's crest, *maru-ichi* was once painted white. The holes drilled thru the iron plates indicate where cloth tongs would normally be inserted.

CLOG MAKER

PLATE 44

43 × 20 × 13 cm. (17 × 8 × 5 in.)
Meiji Period
Museum of Ishikawa Prefecture, Kanazawa
Lacquered wood and cloth
Mozō KANBAN

A shop in Kanazawa, at the end of the Meiji period, used these more elaborate and refined *geta* to advertise its wares. The lacquer is done in a style known as *Kaga maki-e*, a tradition of lacquer technique and decoration that has been passed down within the Igarashi family of Kanazawa from the mid-seventeenth century. Kanazawa was one of the major cultural centers of Japan and supported an aristocracy that could afford such luxuries. *Sakurai chōsei*, "made by Sakurai," written on the underside of these over-sized geta, makes this one of the very rare signed kanban in this collection.

TABI SHOP

PLATE 45

45 × 60 cm. (17¾ × 23½ in.)
Edo Period
The Hosoda Collection, Tokyo
Polychromed wood
Mokei KANBAN

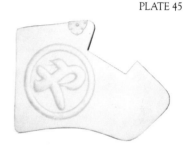

Tabi, the uniquely Japanese, one-toed cotton sock, is the footwear traditionally worn indoors with kimono and *hakama* (the formal attire for men). White cloth is always used for women and for men when dressed in formal attire. Black is for workmen, particularly gardeners. The classic tabi kanban is a *mokei* identified by its shape–the pattern from which the cloth is cut, rather than the finished tabi. A carved crest identified the maker and sometimes a simple word like *daijōbu*, which meant "tough" or "strong" in the Edo period, was added.

SHOE MAKER

PLATE 46

18 × 25.5 cm. (7 × 10 in.)
Taishō Period
Edwin Hewitt, New York
Lacquered wood
Mokei KANBAN

At the turn of the nineteenth century, European high fashion set the tone for the fashion-conscious Japanese upper class. This kanban illustrates the square toe, pierced leather trim and tie over the instep depicted in English and German fashion magazines of the Edwardian period (1901-1910). These details are faithfully reproduced in heavy gold lacquer by a Japanese craftsman just a few years later.

TEXTILE MERCHANT

PLATE 47

131 × 66 cm. (51½ × 34 in.)
Early Edo Period
Shōwa Neon Collection, Tokyo
Wood
Sage KANBAN

Silk material and cotton products were sold by this shop reputed to have been one of the first Mitsui family enterprises, founded in 1675. The words on the right *genkin shōfuda*, "cash only,' price as marked," were a catch phrase coined by Mitsui Hachirōemon in the latter half of the seventeenth century. This kanban is believed also to be of that period. *Santo shiire*, "gathered from three capitals" is inscribed on the left. Usually the three cities referred to were Kyoto, Edo and Naniwa, as Osaka was formerly called. But since cotton cloth came from Nara, it is likely that this reference is to Kyoto, Nara and Naniwa. The shop's name was Kaneki-ya. Horizontal strips of wood at the top and bottom, inserted at a later date, were probably intended to prevent warping of this fine *keyaki* wood sign.

KIMONO SHOP

97 × 55 cm. (38¼ × 21¾ in.)
Edo Period
Peabody Museum of Salem
Polychromed wood
Shōkei kanban

Kanban makers were influenced by contemporary art trends and aesthetics. *Ukiyo-e* prints often provided the subjects and the artistic inspiration could be quite direct, as is the case with this handsome double kanban for a kimono shop (*gofuku-ya*). The courtesan with the long black tresses, stylized eye and attenuated lip area is painted in the style of the Maruyama Shijō school of painting active in the 18th century. The elaborate headdress and heavily patterned kimono of the figure on the other side reflect the fascination with the classic Chinese style. Kimono shops in early 19th century Kyoto were owned by individual merchants, but in Tokyo the forerunners of some of the department store dynasties were already operating as gofuku-ya.

FAN SHOP

160 × 90 cm. (63 × 35½ in.)
Late Meiji/Taishō Period
The Hosoda Collection, Tokyo
Paper, bamboo
Mozō kanban

The fan shape, *ōgi-gata,* is used on signboards either for its symbolic connotations or to advertise a fan shop. Although this brightly painted paper and bamboo model is a *sensu* or folding fan, larger rigid frame fans for dancing, called *uchiwa,* were probably also sold in this shop. Custom made fans were available at this wholesale, *oroshi,* shop: "If you want your own design, it will be acceptable," is written on the reverse side.

WIG MAKER

44 × 33 cm. (17¼ × 13 in.)
Edo Period
Kenichi Higasa Collection, Kobe
Polychromed wood
Mokei kanban

Wigmaker's signs of this type were common in the 18th and 19th centuries. The *keyaki* wood, chosen for its durability, is inscribed with *kazura,* (wig) on one side and *kazura-han* on the other. In the Kansai region, *han* often replaced *san* as the honorific for a name, so this becomes something of a play on words–"Mr. Wig-man." This kanban illustrates a man's wig in traditional samurai hair style.

SHOP FOR HAIR ORNAMENTS

30.4 × 7.6 cm. (12 × 3 in.)
Edo Period
The Hosoda Collection, Tokyo
Polychromed wood
Mokei kanban

Lacquer, mother of pearl, jade, and boxwood hair pins like this oversize replica, adorned the elaborate coiffures of ladies in the Edo period. The "three-comma" crest is frequently selected for its design quality rather than its symbolic or familial associations. The little heart-shaped piece at the top was used for cleaning the ears.

PLATE 48 PLATE 49 PLATE 50. PLATE 51.

UMBRELLA SHOP

PLATE 52

28 × 10 cm. (11 × 4 in.)
Edo Period
Minezō Tani, Tokyo
Polychromed wood
MOKEI KANBAN

This kanban simulates an umbrella made of bamboo and oiled paper and relies on its shape to identify the shop. Not a stroke of writing is used on it. The dating of this piece is confirmed by the thick coating of *aka-urushi,* a type of lacquer in common use during the Edo period. Collapsible umbrellas of this type were first made at the end of the Momoyama period.

COMB SHOP

PLATE 53

45 × 48 cm. (17¾ × 19 in.)
Edo Period
The Hosoda Collection, Tokyo
Wood
MOKEI KANBAN

A play on words animates this easily recognized kanban for a *kushi-ya* or comb maker's shop. The radical *ku* of *kushi* has two readings—"suffering" and the number nine. *Shi* also has two readings—"death" and the number four. The association with death makes four an unlucky number in Japan which shares the Western phobia of thirteen. Taking the numerical readings of *ku* and *shi,* 9 and 4, a comb-maker in Kyoto in the early Edo period cleverly chose the luckier combination of 10 (*jū*) and 3 (*san*) to make thirteen and called his shop *Jūsan-ya.* Many shops that sell combs adopted the luckier *Jūsan-ya* and this form, although an anachronism, is still seen today. The original Jūsan-ya is still in existence in Kyoto.

This design of this comb is stylized but based on the utilitarian short-toothed, square wooden comb that was in common use during the Edo period. More elaborate combs were used by courtesans for decorative purposes.

The very graphic crest is a simplified visual hieroglyph of two mountains combined with the *katakana* character *sa.* It is read *yamasa,* a common term for businesses.

SHOP FOR BUDDHIST PRAYER BEADS

PLATE 54

Length 227 cm. (90 in.)
Mid-Edo Period
Ōmiya Nakano Isuke Shōten, Kyoto
Wood and silk
JITSUBUTSU KANBAN

Buddhist prayer beads varied in size, length and the number of beads strung. Some are meant to be handled like rosaries, others are worn by pilgrims or members of the Buddhist clergy over their robes as an accessory, as those shown here. Buddhist prayer beads are made of everything from common hardwood to gemstones. During the Edo period *juzu* shops proliferated and specialized only in beads, which were bought as souvenirs by the pilgrims to Kyoto, the capital of Buddhism in Japan and site of more than a thousand temples. Today these shops also sell Buddhist robes, portable shrines and other objects of devotion.

This string of *keyaki* wood beads with its silk tassel has been used·at Ōmiya Nakano Isuke Shōten on Teramachi Street in Kyoto since its founding in 1764.

PLATE 55

SHOP FOR BUDDHIST PRAYER BEADS
84 × 40 cm. (33 × 15½ in.)
Mid-Edo Period
Ōmiya Nakano Isuke Shōten, Kyoto
Polychromed wood
YANE KANBAN

This string of Buddhist prayer beads (*nenju* or *juzu*), hung from a hole pierced in a *keyaki* board, was the first kanban used by the Ōmiya family when its business opened in 1794. It illustrates the shorter form of beads which were handled more than they were worn. The characters carved in the upper corners of the kanban advertise "*karaki* wood from India"–identifying India, the scene of Buddha's enlightenment, with the wood gives it special value.

This *yane* kanban was also hung by the Ōmiya Nakano Isuke Shōten and reflects the old Kyoto architectural style. Although the structure was built by a master carpenter, the sign itself was usually carved by a kanban maker. The beads set within the lobed silhouette are a particularly graceful design.

THE MARTIAL ARTS

PLATE 56

HELMET MAKER
74 × 65 cm. (29 × 25½ in.)
Early Edo Period
Peabody Museum of Salem
Polychromed wood
MOZŌ KANBAN

The tradition of helmets and armor reached a high degree of design and stylization in the Momoyama period, when they were still in use. During the Edo period when the country was at peace, helmets were designed more as elements of ceremonial costume than utilitarian objects. This example of a classic warrior's helmet is carved in wood to resemble metal and elaborately corded silk. Horns, dragon and crests have been carved and painted red, green, black and gold.

PLATE 57

SCABBARD MAKER
66.8 × 27 cm. (26¼ × 10½ in.)
Late Edo Period
Peabody Museum of Salem
Sharkskin, metal and lacquer
SHŌKEI KANBAN

This kanban for *saya*, decorative sword scabbards, advertises another specialized skill in the fine Japanese art of sword-making. Here samples of scabbards made from sharkskin, *hiramaki-e* and *nashiji* lacquer ware, and wood inlaid with mother-of-pearl are displayed in a lacquered frame with fine metal fittings. This sign was visible from either direction when hung perpendicular to the shop facade.

SHOP FOR A SWORD HILT WRAPPER
PLATE 58

60 × 30 cm. (23½ × 11¾ in.)
Edo Period
The Hosoda Collection, Tokyo
Metal, leather, sharkskin, wood
NOKIZURI KANBAN

The skills of several craftsmen were required to make a fine sword. The blade, sword guard, hilt, *menuki* (decorative metal fittings), and grip wrapping required specialized skills in gold and silver, lacquer and leather. The art of sword-grip wrapping, *tsukamaki,* is advertised by this kanban. Nakabayashi, the shop owner, will "prepare long swords or short" and "accept old swords for repair or in exchange of money."

These craftsmen covered the wooden base of the hilt with several layers of material—sharkskin, silk, lacquered cloth or leather. More than seventy styles of wrapping the hilt with silk macrame cording are known. Distinctions of rank of the samurai, social class, or geographic location are indicated by the design. The grip-wrapping represented on this kanban is a design originally from Kyūshū. Carrying swords in public was officially outlawed in 1874 and swords became principally ceremonial objects after that time.

SCHOOL FOR THE MARTIAL ARTS
PLATE 59

Diameter 47 cm. (18½ in.)
Edo Period
Shōwa Neon Collection, Tokyo
Wood and iron
MOKEI KANBAN

Visual and verbal puns were a favorite device of the kanban maker, often compensating for lavish materials banned by the sumptuary laws. This sign for a school teaching martial arts falls in this category, but its meaning is a little obtuse. It combines three symbols—the sickle (*kama*), the circle (*wa*), and the *hiragana* character *nu.* *Kamawanu* is a colloquial expression of casual greeting or informal welcome. The message intended by the martial arts studio may have been "Enter at your own risk." The *kama-wa-nu* design was adapted as a *maneki,* welcoming, symbol often used on *noren.*

Visually this kanban is rustic and understated in the best Japanese style. Long, old-fashioned, iron nails and the metal symbols for *kama wa nu* are mounted on a circle of weathered, worm-eaten wood. On the back two vertical grooves about an inch wide divide the circle to prevent warping.

ARROW MAKER
PLATE 60

103 × 65 cm. (40½ × 25½ in.)
Mid-Edo Period
The Hosoda Collection, Tokyo
Wood and metal
JITSUBUTSU KANBAN

Eight wooden arrows are framed and inset in this two-sided kanban from the early 1800s. *Onyōkyū-shi,* meaning "bow and arrow master craftsman" is written down the center, and the name of the master, Fujiwara Tadashige, is on the left. These arrows were not used by the samurai for fighting but were intended strictly for the sport of archery which was very popular among the upper classes.

PLATE 61.

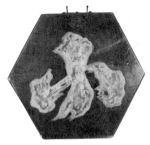

MONEY LENDER
41 × 45 cm. (16 × 18 in.)
Edo Period
The Hosoda Collection, Tokyo
Polychromed wood
SAGE KANBAN

This kanban consists of two signs identical in shape—one with the character *dai*, (large) and one with *shō*, (small). Both moneylenders and pawnshops used signs like this pair throughout the Edo period to indicate the prevailing rate of interest which was prorated for long or short years since the number of months per year varied under the calendar system in use.

Prior to 1873, the Japanese used a lunisolar calendar, *taiin taiyō reki*, which they had modified from the Chinese. According to this lunar calendar, most years alternated between "big" months of thirty days and "little" months of twenty-nine—a total of 366 days for the year. However, seven years out of every nineteen were leap years, which had a thirteenth month of thirty days—a total of 396 days. The adoption of the western calendar in January 1873 obviated the need for signs like this, and they became historical curiosities.

PLATE 62.

ABACUS SHOP
131 × 50 cm. (51¼ × 19¾ in.)
Meiji/Taishō Period
The Hosoda Collection, Tokyo
Wood
JITSUBUTSU KANBAN

This is the perfect example of a *jitsubutsu* kanban. It is oversized and was hung vertically but otherwise is a perfect replica of the abacus, which is the piece of equipment most widely used by all merchants and tradesmen in Japan. The *soroban* (abacus) first came to Japan from China in the 15th century and its design has remained virtually unchanged through the centuries. This kanban is a particularly refined piece of carving. The frame and disks are cherry, wood usually reserved for fine woodwork.

PLATE 63

MONEY LENDER
35.5 × 140 cm. (14 × 55 in.)
Edo Period
Mrs. Marian Hammer, Bigorio, Switzerland
Painted tin on wood
NOKIZURI KANBAN

This kanban for a gold and silver moneylender documents one role of the Tokugawa Shogunate in the nascent banking industry. At the beginning of their rule (1600-1868), the Shogunate founded a silver mint, the Ginza, located on the site of the famous street of the same name in contemporary Tokyo. Early in the 17th century, the Kinza, a gold mint, was opened at the present site of the Bank of Japan in downtown Tokyo. The Shogunate permitted certain families to lend these precious metals as money and used the profits to fund civic needs.

The silver piece on the right commemorates an auspicious day on New Year's, 1587, when this family was commissioned by the Shogun to raise money for the expense of "guarding the castle" and "maintaining the army." In recognition of service, this family was permitted to use the three-leafed hollyhock Tokugawa crest.

The gold piece on the left records a later commission, in 1793, to raise money for the "traveling expenses of the conquering army."

The shape of the money exchange symbol derives from an ancient weight used to calculate the value of precious metals and became the recognized mark of a banking institution.

PAWNSHOP

PLATE 64

14 × 12 cm. (5½ × 4¾ in.)
Edo Period
The Hosoda Collection, Tokyo
Lacquer on wood
MOKEI KANBAN

Shōgi, the popular Japanese equivalent of chess, is played with markers differentiated not by shape but by the *kanji* carved on the piece. The character inscribed may be *ōshō* (king) or, as here, *kaku,* a wild pawn. The kaku first moves across the board diagonally, but in a certain position is turned over and becomes "gold," the most powerful piece on the board. A kaku was also an Edo period coin and the game of shōgi was popularly associated with money, partially from prizes and gambling.

The shape of the shōgi pawn was adopted as a pawn shop symbol for these reasons although the English pun does not exist in the Japanese. The shōgi shape, inscribed with either a proper name or the word *yagō* (literally, "name of a shop") indicated a pawnshop; kanji for a chess rank or piece signalled a place where chess pieces were made or where the game was played. Because kaku was both a coin and a chess rank, the meaning of this sign is ambiguous, but evidence supports the pawnshop designation.

COIN EXCHANGE

PLATE 65

Diameter 28 cm. (11 in.)
Edo Period
Minezō Tani, Tokyo
Wood, lacquer
MOKEI KANBAN

In the field of money and banking, certain kanban designs became widely accepted with the rise of the merchant class under the Tokugawas. This sign for a coin money changer was primarily used by small money exchangers rather than large banks.

The design for the kanban comes from the Chinese copper coins which the Japanese adopted during the Kanei era of Edo (1624-1644). The four characters on the face of the coin read from top to bottom and right to left, *Kanei tsūhō,* literally, "currency of the Kanei era."

STATIONERY SHOP

PLATE 66

61.5 × 27 cm. (24¼ × 10½ in.)
Meiji Period
The Hosoda Collection, Tokyo
Painted wood
MOZŌ KANBAN

Account books were sold by a *chōmen-ya,* or stationery shop. "Daifukuchō" was a very popular brand during the second half of the nineteenth century and its kanban were frequently seen. This painted wood version dates from the Meiji period. In the late Edo period, account book kanban were given a realistic form by stretching heavy paper over a bamboo frame shaped like a notebook. These signs traditionally hung above the first roof from a bamboo tree or a branch and were changed every New Year—a clean sign to advertise a clean slate of account books for the new fiscal year.

An *ukiyo-e* print by an unknown Edo artist (Figure 1) shows how the kanban were displayed in a busy shop. In the print, we glimpse the shop of a Mr. Iida whose business is part of a chain of shops called *Kawachi-ya.* The print indicates that many kinds of account books were sold—income records or balance sheets, account books for "happy occasions" and even ones for funerals. Along the upper gables of the roof are the symbols for Fukurokuju, one of the Seven Happy Gods who is especially worshipped by merchants for property protection. His name combines "happiness" *(fuku),* "riches" *(roku),* and "longevity" *(ju).*

149

Kanban for medicine or medical services form the largest category of signs extant. The majority of these signs were made in the Meiji era, particularly after 1884 when a law was passed requiring the registration of trademarks, *tōroku shōhyō*. The first three trademarks registered under this act were for medical products. Signs made prior to 1884 use a less formal authorization.

The owners of a trademark for a product—a patent medicine, for example—began to create a retail distribution, licensing shops throughout the country to sell a product exclusively. Broad-base advertising of brand name products began to replace unique signs for family-managed stores and services. Kanban were produced in quantity in the home office and then distributed to the retail outlets, who added their shop name to the sign and personalized them in other ways. Medical kanban by necessity use more calligraphy to explain the virtues of the product, but literacy was also more common in the Meiji period.

The "Chūjōtō" brand medicine, still popular today, has been produced since the early Meiji period by Tsumura Juntendō from a formula ascribed to the legendary Princess Chūjō. According to the Heian epic, *Chūjō Hime Monogatari*, Princess Chūjō of the ruling Fujiwara family had many romantic troubles and eventually became a nun at Taima-dera in Nara, a temple famed for the import of Chinese products and a training center in Chinese herbal medicine.

A Heian-style princess has been used consistently to advertise "Chūjōtō" brand medicine, although the design has been altered successively over the years. The first Heian-style headdress and robe of the Princess Chūjō trademark was painted by an unknown artist and was already well known when it was registered as the Tsumura Juntendō trademark in 1903. (See Plates 70-72.) The current version painted in 1922 by Kei Takabata, a popular portraitist of Meiji beauties, is an abstraction of the original trademark.

By linguistic coincidence, the word *chūjō*, written with different kanji, has other associations with women's medical treatment. The first Japanese gynecologist was Chūjō Tatewaki, doctor to the women in the household of the great Toyotomi Hideyoshi (1536-1598). In early Meiji, the words *Chūjō-ryū fujin ryōji* (Chūjō-style women's clinics) were used on small kanban for abortion clinics and the term is still in current usage in Japan.

PLATE 67

PHARMACY SIGN FOR STOMACH MEDICINE
90 × 30 cm. (35½ × 12 in.)
Meiji Period
The Hosoda Collection, Tokyo
Polychromed wood
SAGE KANBAN

Kanban for the same medical product did not always have the same design—as illustrated by the comparison between these signs for a stomach medicine called *Uruyusu*. The Dutch name Vloym Van Mittr and the Japanese words "licensed from Holland" featured prominently on this kanban were good advertising in the Meiji era which prized foreign products. This sign, like those of modern-day Japan, combines four alphabets—the Roman, *kanji*, *hiragana*, and *katakana*, the script usually used to transliterate foreign words. The description of the medicine is on the right and the address of the main store in Osaka is on the left. Kanban of this design were located in various parts of Japan, lending credence to the theory that this was the official sign, distributed to licensed retail shops.

The diamond trademark uses an abstract three-branched pine crest, symbolic of strength, endurance and longevity. See Plate 88 for comparison.

PHARMACY SIGN FOR STOMACH MEDICINE

PLATE 68

80 × 110.5 cm. (31½ × 43½ in.)
Meiji Period
Peabody Museum of Salem
Polychromed wood
Shōkei kanban

This unique kanban for the Van Mittr medicine is more flamboyant. A foreign gentleman in a top hat gallops on a golden steed to the rescue of anyone with stomach cramps. The sign he carries romanizes the name of the medicine as *Uluus*, but the calligraphy is identical to the *Uruyusu* in *katakana* on the previous Van Mittr sign (Plate 67). The name of the Osaka pharmacy, Matsuo Kenjudō, and its seal, are also legible. Both sides of the sign are identical and legible from either direction. Apparently original signs were acceptable advertisement even for products which had an officially licensed kanban.

EYE MEDICINE SIGN

PLATE 69

37 × 98 cm. (14½ × 38½ in.)
Meiji Period
Shōwa Neon Collection, Tokyo
Polychromed wood
Shōkei kanban

Sailboats incised in wood drift across a ground of tarnished gold and silver in this elegant sign for a brand of eye medicine. On the left sail, is modestly written the claim, "God's medicine" *(Shinyaku)*. The brand name "Ippōsui" is comprised of characters reading "one direction" and "water," whose meaning is illustrated by the motif of two sailboats floating on water.

The Ippōsui brand was a patent medicine manufactured by Shiseidō, now one of the largest cosmetics firms in the world, and licensed for sale at this shop, Mitamura Yakuho. Several contemporary Japanese corporations started as pharmacies, including the illustrious Sumitomo banking family. (See Figure 7.)

PHARMACY SIGN FOR WOMEN'S AILMENTS

PLATE 70

136 × 46 cm. (53½ × 18 in.)
Meiji Period
Kenichi Higasa Collection, Kobe
Polychromed wood
Shōkei kanban

This two-sided kanban for "Chūjōtō" brand patent medicine features the Heian Princess wearing Edo-style kimono on both sides. This sign predates the trademark registration of 1884, and merely states the name of the manufacturer, Tsumura Juntendō, and the address of the Tokyo office. Again, the medicine is touted for "female complaints" and "womb disease."

PLATE 71

PHARMACY SIGN FOR "CHŪJŌTŌ" AND "IKATSU" MEDICINES
Diameter 103 cm. (40½ in.)
Meiji Period
Sue Chōritsu Hakubutsukan
Polychromed wood
SAGE KANBAN

The round shape of this kanban for "Chūjōtō" medicine is distinctive, but a similar shape appears in a newspaper clipping dated July 19, 1908 from the Tsumura Juntendō company files. This sign was obviously exposed to the elements and was not taken in each night, in contrast to the following plate which dates from the same time but which had the side handles for easy transport. This sign advertises, "good medicine for women" and identifies the shop as "Chiyo-yakkyoku" outside of Fukuoka near the village of Sue.

The stomach medicine "Ikatsu," licensed by Tsumura Juntendō in 1908, is advertised on the reverse side of this sign. The foreigner in the top hat and bow tie who represents this product bears a certain resemblance to "Mr. Help" (Plate 72) and is an early example of the rendering of a Western subject in the style of Western realism.

PLATE 72

PHARMACY SIGN FOR "HELP" AND "CHŪJŌTŌ" MEDICINES
121 × 38 cm. (47½ × 15 in.)
Meiji Period
Takahashi-shi Shiryōkan
Polychromed wood, metal
SAGE KANBAN

"Chūjōtō," the drug on which the Tsumura Juntendō empire was founded, was traditionally included on all signboards produced by the company. Here, the Princess Chūjō is depicted with the Heian-style headdress to advertise this cure for gynecological distress. The instructions are succinct: "Women's hysteria medicine. Mix with water."

This sign advertising two medicines hung in the village of Takahashi in Okayama-ken on a pharmacy founded in the latter part of the Edo period, circa 1800. The shop did business in Takahashi until about twenty years ago and, when it closed, the kanban was presented to the town museum. Permission for this sign to come to the United States was voted by the Town Council.

The Tsumura Juntendō pharmaceutical company expanded its line of products at the turn of the century and were licensed to sell the stomach medicine, "Help," in 1908. The dapper gentleman in the derby fits the Meiji image of the Westerner and the English name, "Help," in both Roman lettering and transliterated in *katakana,* is intended not as humor but to convey that this medicine is truly the most recent medical find. The remedy is effective for disorders of the stomach and the intestine, such as diarrhea.

PLATE 73

PHARMACY SIGN FOR MENSTRUAL CRAMP MEDICINE
37 × 29 cm. (14½ × 11½ in.)
Meiji/Taishō Period
Private Collection
Polychromed wood
SAGE KANBAN

This fancifully painted kanban designed to appeal to the young girl advertises "Gettsūgan," a medicine claimed "especially effective for menstrual problems." The rendering of angels and the heart shape, which document the introduction of Western cliches into Japanese popular culture, date this sign.

PHARMACY SIGN FOR MOTHERS' MEDICINE

PLATE 74

42 × 91.5 cm. (16½ × 36 in.)
Meiji/Taishō Period
Mr. and Mrs. Michael Thorman, Oakland
Polychromed wood
SAGE KANBAN

This polychromed carved kanban which features a kimono-clad nursing mother cleverly combines two medicines—one for mother and one for child. The medicine for the mother, "Blodomosu" is a treatment for the womb and "cleans the blood system." "Kenjigan" for the baby promises "detoxification" and cure for infant eczema. Tanikawa Seishōdō is the maker whose head office is in Kōchi, Shikoku. The word *Kaden* means "secret formula." The Roman lettering on this sign is a decidedly Meiji touch, as is the ornate scroll design.

PHARMACY SIGN FOR A PATENT MEDICINE

PLATE 75

76 × 56 cm. (30 × 22 in.)
Meiji Period
Becton Dickinson and Company Corporate Art Collection,
Paramus, N.J.
Lacquer on wood, mother-of-pearl
SHŌKEI KANBAN

This highly decorative kanban is in the shape of a Buddhist temple bell displayed with its silk cover or wrapping. It is exquisitely carved with two textures achieved by different methods of applying the lacquer—wiping to reveal the wood grain on the surface of the bell and stipling for the silk wrapping. The mother-of-pearl inset on the "three comma crest" is elegant.

The subject of this intricate sign is a "fragrant iron pill," the Japanese equivalent of Lydia Pinkham's Pills or Carter's Little Liver Pills. The columns of *kanji* on the lower half of the sign list a broad spectrum of ills for which it is effective: for poverty of blood in both adults and children; for weak digestion; pain in the stomach and sour stomach; for hysterics before and after childbirth; for uterine disease, dropsy and beriberi; for greensickness, and weakness.

EYEGLASS SHOP

PLATE 76

24 × 30 cm. (9½ × 11¾ in.)
Meiji Period
Dr. Wynant Dean, Louisville, Ky.
Polychromed wood, glass
MOKEI KANBAN

The popularity of *megane,* eyeglasses, in the Meiji era cannot be attributed entirely to universally poor Japanese eyesight. Eyeglasses had become fashionable. They were first introduced to Japan by Francis Xavier, missionary and founder of the Jesuit order who also brought binoculars, musical instruments, watches and mirrors as gifts. Glasses were first made in Japan during the Genna period (1615-1624) by a craftsman who learned the technique in Malaya. By the end of the Edo period, many shops sold new eyeglasses, bought old pairs to refurbish and resell, and repaired glasses. During the Meiji period such shops prospered. A Japanese was sent by the government to the Vienna Exposition of 1873 to learn the latest techniques.

PLATE 77

PHARMACY SIGN FOR EYE MEDICINE
119 × 35.5 cm. (47 × 14½ in.)
Meiji Period
Mr. and Mrs. Richard Lanier, New York
Polychromed wood
SAGE KANBAN

The vertical shape of this graphic sign for "German Eye Medicine," written in *kanji* down the center, imitates a medicine jar with an eyedropper. The stopper becomes the hat of the person painted peering from the bottle. This sign hung in the shop of Kishimoto Keizō in Osaka after 1884.

PLATE 78

PHARMACY SIGN FOR "JINTAN" STOMACH MEDICINE
60 × 32 cm. (23½ × 12½ in.)
Taishō Period
Takayama City Kyōdokan, Takayama
Polychromed wood
SAGE KANBAN

Patent medicines were the first products to attain a national image through advertising in Japan. The naval officer trademark of "Jintan," a medicine for upset stomach, has been used consistently and successfully for generations and still commands instant recognition. The kanban for "Jintan," a household remedy since Meiji days, lent an aura of stability to a pharmacy and was reassuring, especially to older clients. Retail shops licensed to sell the product were given this kanban by the drug manufacturer who thus retained control of his product image. This example once hung in front of a pharmacy in Takayama and dates from the Taishō era (1912-1926). The faint white lettering reads "pocket-sized" and "good for the stomach."

PLATE 79

PHARMACY SIGN FOR RHEUMATISM REMEDY
35.5 × 63.5 cm. (14 × 25 in.)
Meiji Period
Herbert Hemphill, Jr., New York
Polychromed wood
SAGE KANBAN

The wild boar trademark on this Japanese Pinocchio makes this one of the most humorous kanban, although it is quite possible that its creator had no intention of being funny. Its artistic interest is derived from its cartoon quality. A lot of information had to be fitted into a small space: that this medicine is good medicine for various kinds of rheumatism (transliterated in *katakana* as *ryū-machi-su*), particularly the "poisonous" and "fungoid" varieties. The re-assuring advertising slogan is *zen-chi,* meaning that if you take this you will completely recover. The boar is the registered trademark of Anjū Shōkai whose home office is in Osaka.

PHARMACY SIGN FOR COLD REMEDY

PLATE 80

126 × 33 cm. (49½ × 13 in.)
Mid-Edo Period
Minezō Tani, Tokyo
Polychromed wood
SAGE KANBAN

Artist friends or patrons sometimes painted a kanban for a merchant and produced signs of high artistic quality. This rather rustic and undistinguished sign is ascribed to Ike no Taiga (1723-1776), one of the foremost painters of the Nanga School of the 18th century. He was known as both a calligrapher and a painter. The *rakugo-ka*, comedian story tellers whose art documented the history and ethics of the merchant class in the Edo period, relate that Ike no Taiga designed this kanban in gratitude to a druggist whose special medicine cured a bad cold. The word *hollander* under the crest indicates that Aka Bannōkō, "almighty cream," was made from a Dutch formula by the druggist Inoue of Kyoto.

The crest designed by Ike no Taiga was registered as a trademark after 1870 when the medicine was sold throughout the country. A later but similar version of this kanban from The Hosoda Collection shows two revisions: the words for registered trademark have been added and the reference to the Dutch formula has been dropped.

PHARMACY SIGN FOR STOMACH MEDICINE

PLATE 81

83 × 43.5 cm. (32½ × 17 in.)
Edo Period
Peabody Museum of Salem
Polychromed wood
SHŌKEI KANBAN

This dramatic kanban is a carving of the classic Japanese depiction of the devil with grimace, horns and clawed hands and feet. The Japanese saying *"Oni ni kanabo,"* which means "A demon with an iron club," and conjures the image of brute strength, is implied. This sign is a fine example of folk art carving.

The kanban advertises a particular brand of stomach pain medicine "Kumanoi Mokkōgan" which literally means "Bear's Gall Wood–fragrance Pills." Bear's gall is a Japanese herbal medicine, known to have been used as early as the 13th century when it was mentioned in the famous epic, *The Tales of Heike.*

PHARMACY SIGN FOR KIDNEY MEDICINE

PLATE 82

142 × 54 cm. (56 by 21 in.)
Edo Period
Shōwa Neon Collection, Tokyo
Lacquered wood
SAGE KANBAN

One of the principal sources for the documentation of kanban–how and when they were used–is *ukiyo-e* and other prints in which signs are part of the scenery. A similar kanban is pictured in an ukiyo-e print by an unknown artist, circa 1850 (Figure 19). The print clearly answers one puzzle–how an elaborately lacquered sign could be preserved although it was hung outdoors. Here we see that in addition to its own little roof, shutters protected it from the elements at night. The dating of this kanban is verified by the use of the Imperial chrysanthemum crest which would not have been permitted in the Meiji era without alteration (as in Plate 13). Listed on the sign are various herbs purported to be effective for kidney ailments, such as dragon's eye.

PLATE 83.

CHIROPRACTOR

Diameter 78 cm. (30¾ in.)
Edo Period
Kenichi Higasa Collection, Kobe
Polychromed wood, metal
SAGE KANBAN

This handsome kanban was hung by a chiropractor who utilized the medicine "Seikotsu-Kō" in his practice. It was a "miracle" drug concocted by herb doctors to cure "headaches, sore shoulder, toothache, hemorrhoids and bruises." The chiropractor advocated its use as a "bone fixing plaster" to set fractures.

Above the crest is the word *kankyo,* "authorized by the government," which indicates that this sign was made before registration of trademarks was instituted in 1884. The dark green painted surface is highlighted with gold lacquer lettering and fine metal work.

PLATE 84

PHARMACY SIGN FOR CHINESE HERBAL MEDICINE

114 × 36 cm. (53 × 15 in.)
Edo Period
The Hosoda Collection, Tokyo
Lacquered wood
SAGE KANBAN

The quality of the lacquer and sweep of the calligraphy are the outstanding features of this kanban for a Chinese herbal medicine known as "Jiōgan." *Gan,* meaning "rounded shape" is a suffix often used to designate a medicine in pill form. "Jiōgan" was a form of spice which was sold in "six tastes" or "eight flavors" and, as a tonic, was purported to have aphrodisiacal benefits. A Chinese medicine shop sold herbs for cooking as well as herbs for medicinal purposes.

PLATE 85

PHARMACY SIGN FOR PAIN-KILLER

80 × 60 cm. (31½ × 23½ in.)
Meiji Period
Kenichi Higasa Collection, Kobe
Lacquer on wood
MOKEI KANBAN

The shape of this handsome lacquered kanban is the mallet which is an attribute of Daikoku, one of the Seven Gods of Fortune, who is traditionally depicted carrying a hammer in his right hand and with a bag slung over his left shoulder. It advertises a pain-killer for which the invocation of the folk religious image had comforting connotations. The central three characters are rendered in an archaic script unlike the formal calligraphy exhibited elsewhere on this kanban. The two-bird registered trademark is a lyrical addition to the design.

PLATE 86

PHARMACY SIGN

121 × 39 cm. (47½ × 15½ in.)
Meiji Period
National Institute of Japanese Literature,
Division of Historical Documents, Tokyo
Polychromed wood
SHŌKEI KANBAN

This very ornate kanban is almost baroque in its use of gold and its elaborate imagery borrowed from *ukiyo-e* prints. This decorative sign portrays a lady dressed in extremely formal kimono, reading a hand scroll. The carving and painting of a complicated image, commonly rendered in prints and paintings, indicates the great artistry of the sign maker. The dramatically raised gold crest is a striking graphic symbol.

INN AT A FERRYBOAT LANDING

PLATE 87

158 × 23 cm. (62½ × 9 in.)
Early Edo Period
Kanichirō Ueda, Kyoto Mingeikan
Polychromed wood
MOKEI KANBAN

From 1630, this weathered kanban shaped like a boat paddle hung in front of an inn on the banks of the Yodo River in Fushimi. Fushimi was the northern terminus of the ferry that plied the busy route between Kyoto and Naniwa (Osaka). The river teemed with life and all sorts of goods were hawked along its banks. Especially famous were the dishes of food, known as *kura wanka,* served in Imari bowls to the passengers. The ferry was named the *Sanjikkoku-bune,* literally "thirty measures of rice," from the capacity of the boat which held thirty travelers and five crewmen.

BATHHOUSE

PLATE 88

39 × 104 cm. (15½ × 41 cm.)
Edo Period
Museum of Ishikawa Prefecture, Kanazawa
Polychromed wood
MOKEI KANBAN

This late Edo period kanban advertised a bathhouse in the town of Kanazawa. The characters, written in an archaic style, read *matsu no yu,* (literally, "pine-heated water"). Matsu no yu was frequently used as a bathhouse name since the pine tree was the emblem of strength, endurance and longevity. According to legend, the sap of the pine tree runs freely for a thousand years before it turns to amber. This kanban borrows the important lucky symbol of the umbrella pine tree to convey its message. The well-weathered cedar has remnants of orange and green paint.

INCENSE SHOP

PLATE 89

150 × 58 cm. (59 × 23 in.)
Early Edo Period
The Hosoda Collection, Tokyo
Polychromed wood and silk
SHŌKEI KANBAN

The rare Momoyama and early Edo period kanban that have survived fire and destruction are mainly simple reproductions of objects or their containers. This seventeenth century kanban for incense is an early example of the more elaborate gold-lacquered signs produced in later periods. The heavily decorated Chinoiserie frame conveyed exotic sophistication in the seventeenth century.

This sign belonged to an incense importer, the Kōshūya, in a village in Ōmi, present-day Shiga prefecture. During the latter years of the Momoyama period (1586-1591), the great Hideyoshi maintained his castle at Fushimi near Omi. This shop provided incense for the daimyo's household needs and advertised this fact prominently. Both the Hideyoshi crest and the words *Fushimi goyō* ("in the service of Hideyoshi") appear on the sign. The inscription, "New incense from China," is a euphemism for "foreign" since much of the incense came from India.

The hairstyle and dress of the lady pictured is typical of itinerant fragrance vendors of the Momoyama period, but the sign itself was probably commissioned in early Edo by a later generation of this family, still proud of the Hideyoshi family connection and aware of its commercial potential.

The techniques used to make this kanban are quite elaborate and refined: gold and other colors are painted on silk prepared with a sizing made from ground shells.

PLATE 90

THEATRE SIGNS
Diameter 45 cm. (18 in.)
Meiji Period
Takayama City Kyōdokan
Lacquered wood
SHŌKEI KANBAN

This pair of gold lacquered kanban carved in a floral shape flanked the entrance to a theatre in Takayama from the late nineteenth century to the first part of the twentieth. The theatre known as *Kokugikan* was famous for big musical attractions and other popular events including circuses and jugglers. The character on the sign says *koku*.

PLATE 91

TOY SHOP
26 × 33 cm. (10¼ × 13 in.)
Meiji Period
Kenichi Higasa Collection, Kobe
Lacquered wood
SHŌKEI KANBAN

A *daruma* doll and a drum are carved in high relief and coated with thick red lacquer in this appealing sign for a toy shop. The daruma, whose rounded bottom causes him to bounce perpetually back to an upright position, is the most popular Japanese toy and a common symbol for toy stores.

PLATE 92

TRANSPORTATION SERVICE
90 × 32 cm. (36 × 12½ in.)
Early Meiji Period
Nihon Minzoku Shiryōkan, Matsumoto
Polychromed wood
SAGE KANBAN

The first Tokugawa Shogun, Ieyasu (1542-1616), established a countrywide transportation system which included the famous Fifty-three Stages of the Tōkaidō. Other routes were the Nakasendō, Nikkōkaidō, Kōshūkaidō and Ōshūkaidō. A stage-relay system was created which allocated a certain number of men and horses at each stop on the route. These routes were used by feudal lords and their retinue as well as to speed the delivery of mail and official documents. Enterprising merchants established stables of express messengers and nine of them were authorized officially by the Tokugawa government.

This first wave of Japanese travelers created a need for inns—particularly at the relay stations. To insure accommodations for its many messengers, the Domestic Transportation Co. Ltd. organized the most reliable inn at each relay stage into an association. The company booked accommodations at these inns when the traveler made other transport arrangements. The Shinseikō, Union of Hotels, was founded in 1874 and member inns displayed its special kanban. The Shinseikō were lower class inns catering to messengers, merchants and common people, and their business flourished.

This Shinseikō kanban was displayed at an inn on the Nakasendō west of Tokyo. The handsome crest flanked on either side by the roman letter E for Express became the symbol of Naikoku Tsūun in 1875.

Inns for messengers on horseback were outmoded by the coming of the railroads and the Shinseikō disappeared before 1928. Naikoku Tsūun, however, switched to rail transport and eventually became Nippon Express, today the largest rail shippers in Japan. The Shinseikō crest which appears on this kanban was maintained by Nippon Express and remains their corporate symbol.

KITE MAKER

PLATE 93

74.5 × 26 cm. (29½ × 10 in.)
Edo Period
The Kite Museum, Tokyo
Polychromed wood, string
SAGE KANBAN

A wooden string holder and string are embedded in the surface of this delightful kanban for a kite-maker. Kite-making and flying reached their zenith in Japan where for generations it has been enjoyed not only as a sport, but as an area of imaginative artistic achievement.

KITE MAKER

PLATE 94

60 × 96 cm. (23½ × 38 in.)
Edo Period
The Hosoda Collection, Tokyo
Painted silk, wood
MOKEI KANBAN

The use of the fan shape, a felicitous symbol, did not necessarily indicate a fan shop or a fan-maker. The old characters for fan are read *suehiro*, from *sue* (end) and *hirogari* (wide open). This rendering of fan (literally, "in the end all will be possible") indicates the origin of the fan shape as a lucky omen.

ANTIQUE SHOP

PLATE 95

61 × 91 cm. (24 × 36 in.)
Edo/Meiji Period
Tsunehiro Tezuka, Matsumoto
Wood
NIKAI YANEKANBAN

The decorative function of this kanban is evident in its elaborate carving of dragons, cranes, clouds and other fortuitous symbols. Originally it would have harmonized with the architecture of the building. Such detailed and skilled carved wooden signs were executed by master craftsmen to complement the architectural plan.

The carved frame was made in the Edo period, but the central panel was altered later. The writing designates the store as an antique shop. This kanban is still used on a Matsumoto antique shop.

DOLL SHOP OR TEA HOUSE

PLATE 96

125 × 36 cm. (49¼ × 14¼ in.)
Late Edo Period
Kanichirō Ueda, Kyoto Mingeikan
Polychromed wood
SHŌKEI KANBAN

The population of the "floating world," chronicled by the *ukiyo-e* arts of the Edo period, were popular figures and trendsetters. Geisha, sumo wrestlers and Kabuki actors were adopted by enterprising merchants to advertise products of all sorts.

No calligraphy identifies the original use of this sign, but the figures are carefully drawn in vibrant colors. On one side, two courtesans are shaded by an umbrella held by a male attendant. The characters on the back of the smaller woman, *Murasaki Tayū*, indicate the rank of the courtesan. An unidentified sumo wrestler and a famous *tsukebito*, boy wrestler, are depicted on the opposite side. The smaller figure is Daidōzan Bungorō who made sumo history by wrestling at the age of seven in the tournaments of 1794.

Two theories are offered in explanation of this beautiful kanban. Its present owner believes that it hung on a teahouse in Shimabara, the Kyoto pleasure quarter, frequented by the denizens of the "floating world." But it is identified in a history of kanban published thirty years ago with a doll shop famous for its replicas of popular figures.

PLATE 97

BRUSH SHOP
Length 91.4 cm. (36 in.)
Edo Period
Edwin Hewitt, New York
Polychromed wood
Mokei kanban

Brush shops proliferated in the Edo period, catering to the flourishing art of calligraphy which required the finest materials. Brushes were made from hairs of rabbit, badger, goat or horse, selected to meet the needs of the calligrapher or painter. One could buy brushes lighter than a pencil with just a few hairs for detailed work, or ones so large the artist had to stand to use them.

This kanban is stylized, yet represents one of the many kinds and shapes of brushes available in a typical shop. It is so beautifully crafted that it is also a fine piece of sculpture. Identified by its shape, it was probably either suspended in an open frame or hung alone as here. It formerly belonged to Harold Stern, the late curator of the Freer Gallery of Art.

PLATE 98

BRUSH SHOP
143 × 38 cm. (56 × 15 in.)
Mid-Edo Period
Japan Folk Crafts Museum, Tokyo
Polychromed wood
Sage kanban

The illustrated kanban for a brush shop is an early and common type of graphic sign. The earliest known illustration of this type of kanban appears in a scroll from the Muromachi period (1392-1568) recounting the history of Seika-ji. This painted wood sign belonged to a Kyoto brush shop, "Kōrin-dō," named for Ogata Kōrin (1658-1716), the great artist of the Rimpa School. The fluid calligraphy says: "Several schools of Japanese and Chinese writings" on the right and "brushes, ink and inkstones" on the left. The handles on this sign made it easy to transport at closing time.

PLATE 99

PAPER SHOP
184 × 43.3 cm. (72 × 17 in.)
Meiji Period
The Paper Museum, Tokyo
Polychromed wood
Sage kanban

This kanban illustrates the modern chapter in the long history of Japanese paper-making, the importation of Western paper-making machines and techniques in the Meiji period. Paper-making was introduced from China circa 600 AD and the Japanese quickly adapted the techniques and selected three types of bast fiber—the bark of kōzo, gampi and mitsumata plants—still used to make traditional washi (paper). Contrary to popular belief, Japanese paper was never made from rice. Machine-made paper from wood pulp originated in Europe.

The decision of the Emperor Meiji to finance the Kyoto Papierfabrik in 1873 was a radical departure from tradition and typical of his policies of Westernization and modernization. Masanao Makimura, governor of Kyoto prefecture, established Kyoto Papierfabrik with machines and techniques imported from Germany and began wood pulp paper production in Japan. The first mill in Umezu was operated by the Kyoto prefectural government and its construction was directed by a German engineer, Rudolf Lehmann.

This kanban (1879) belonged to Saburō Nakai whose shop sold Kyoto Papierfabrik products. The use of the German words for "pads and fine writing paper" was also in the Meiji tradition of prizing western products.

MUSICAL INSTRUMENTS SHOP

PLATE 100

94 × 30 cm. (37 × 12 in.)
Taishō Period
Kenichi Higasa Collection, Kobe
Painted wood
Mozō kanban

This carving of a violin advertised a music shop for western instruments. It hung under the eaves of the Kusagawa Music Shop. It is a *mozō*, or dummy, kanban, since it could not possibly be played. The instrument is made of light wood and the strings are painted.

TEA HOUSE IN THE GAY QUARTER

PLATE 101

Diameter 79 cm. (31 in.)
Edo Period
Honolulu Academy of Arts
Polychromed wood
Shōkei kanban

The meaning of this kanban is conveyed with exquisite delicacy. It once graced a house in the gay quarter, perhaps in the famous Yoshiwara area during the early Edo period. The courtesan, painted in the style of the famous theatrical painter, Utamaro, has the narrow shoulders and simple hairdo typical of the last decade of the eighteenth century.

An ancient Chinese poem, fraught with complicated literary allusions, is painted on the right. Interpreted with a certain poetic license, the meaning is that beautiful women can lead the nation to ruin, but why shouldn't everyone enjoy the same pleasures as the great rulers? This lady is pointing the way.

GEISHA HOUSE

PLATE 102

61 × 44.5 cm. (24 × 17½ in.)
Meiji Period
Jonathan Whitman, San Francisco
Polychromed wood
Ōiri kanban

The large red double character *ōiri* identifies a type of kanban traditionally given by well-wishers on the opening of a new theatre, restaurant, or inn. The character implies "many people coming." After the opening, the sign is posted to signify that the establishment is sold out.

To this slightly garish sign, given for the opening of a geisha house, the *maneki neko*, the inviting cat and mascot of the demi-monde, was added. This kanban was a gift from a special admirer not only to Kiyomitsu-rō, the geisha house, but also to Etsuko and Rikikichi, whose names are inscribed on the right.

PLATE 103

BOOK-LENDER

30 × 23 cm. (12 × 9 in.)
Edo Period
The Hosoda Collection, Tokyo
Wood
MOKEI KANBAN

This small kanban is in the size and shape of a typical paper-bound book and the design is a replica of a cover. During the Tokugawa period, Japan was isolated from western influences and culture. Only the Dutch East India Company was permitted trade with Japan through its toehold in Nagasaki harbor. Japanese students and scholars flocked to Nagasaki for access to rare Western and Chinese books, usually of a medical or technical nature. These so-called "Dutch studies" made Nagasaki the academic capital of Japan during this period.

This small sign advertised the unusual occupation of a commercial lending library. Books in Japanese, Chinese and Dutch were rented for a fee as the central calligraphy *kashi-hon* (rented books) indicates. This rare and important service gives some sense of the isolation of Japan in the Edo period.

PLATE 104

KABUKI ACTOR'S SIGN

185 × 26 cm. (73 × 10¼ in.)
Meiji Period
Peabody Museum of Salem
Polychromed wood
IORI KANBAN

Kanban connected with the Kabuki theatre form a distinct category. Used for the purpose of announcement rather than selling they, like the *maneki neko* (beckoning cat), have a special place in Japanese life. The use of these *maneki* boards was well-documented by *ukiyo-e* artists of the Kabuki world.

Four different types of kanban were hung by large Kabuki theatres: the *yagura* kanban bearing the name of the theatre; the *ōiri* kanban with its bold red character indicating that the tickets were sold out; the colorful *e* (picture) kanban illustrating scenes from the drama being performed; and the multiple *iori* kanban bearing the names and crests of the actors in the performance.

The type and importance of each kanban is indicated by its design and construction. *Yagura* kanban were permanent fixtures, corporate in design and carefully carved in fine wood. The colorful and stylized *ōiri* kanban were frequently gifts from well-wishers (Plate 102). The temporary but eye-catching *e* kanban were changed for each program and made of paper pasted over wood. These billboard kanban were occasionally supplemented by life-sized dioramas placed on a ledge above the first roof. *Iori* kanban were named for the characteristic "roof" in the shape of the Chinese character meaning *iri,* to enter. The actor's name was written in a full, fluid script called *kabuki-moji,* and bright colors, like the traces of orange and cobalt blue that remain on this sign, were used for the crest.

Iori kanban grew common during the Edo period when established actors traveled the Tōkaidō from Kyoto to Tokyo performing in towns along the way. The narrow width made these signs easy to transport and each actor brought his own. A Kabuki actor would refer proudly to "The day I got my kanban," the equivalent of "The day my name went up in lights." This kanban is for the actor Bandō Ikkaku.

PLATE 105

TOY SHOP

96.3 × 44.5 cm. (38 × 17½ in.)
Meiji Period
Peabody Museum of Salem
Polychromed wood
Mokei kanban

The *daruma* doll sold in every toy shop in Japan was frequently pictured on their kanban. The daruma depicts Bodhidharma, the Indian prince and legendary founder of Zen Buddhism, who according to legend sat in meditation for nine years. When he finally gained enlightenment, he had lost the use of his legs and so he is always depicted with a rounded gourd-like bottom. He is traditionally depicted with a red robe and headdress and with exaggerated Indian features— all attributes of his Indian origin.

By tradition one eye of the daruma is blank until his magic charms help fulfill a wish and the owner may draw in the missing eyeball. Meiji politicians adapted this myth to the worldly arena of campaigning for office and promised that, if elected, they would fill in the eyes of the daruma. Certainly the idea of wishes coming true is appropriate in both politics and toyland. The character on the head of this gaily painted figure is *ōshō,* boss or king in chess.

PLATE 106

MANEKI NEKO (Beckoning Cat)

25.5 × 18 cm. (10 × 7 in.)
Edo Period
Edwin Hewitt, New York
Polychromed wood
Maneki kanban

The *maneki neko,* traditionally portrayed with her left paw raised in the Japanese gesture of beckoning, palm facing out, is a folk symbol instantly recognized by the Japanese. The legend of the maneki neko reveals the moral tone of the merchant society in early Edo. Rival tea houses near the gate of Ekō-in Temple in Tokyo lured customers with beckoning porcelain cats—one golden, the other silver. O-Tsuna, the charming and popular proprietress of the Golden Cat Teahouse, cajoled a large sum of borrowed money from a guest. In debt and remorse, he prepared to throw himself into the Sumida River when he was discovered by O-Tsuna. Told how she had ruined her guest, O-Tsuna joined Hachirobei in committing double suicide. The Golden Cat Teahouse flourished with the success of scandal and eventually the rival house was forced to close.

The tragic legend of feminine wiles and financial disaster appealed to the merchants who adopted the symbolic maneki neko. Replicas in wood, porcelain and paper-mâché are still made. The maneki neko also has a special place in the geisha house (Plate 102).

The beckoning cat was the prototype for a category of *maneki kanban,* which included Fukusuke, *tanuki* (badger) and Okame. They do not sell a particular product or service but are placed at the shop entrance as a lure to customers. This is an early example made of solid wood with touches of color. Sensitively carved, it is an exemplary piece of folk sculpture.

CHRONOLOGY OF JAPANESE HISTORICAL PERIODS

JŌMON	to c. 200 BC
YAYOI	c. 200 BC - c. 250 AD
KOFUN (TUMULUS)	c. 250 - 552
ASUKA	552 - 646
NARA	646 - 794
HEIAN	794 - 1185
KAMAKURA	1185 - 1392
MUROMACHI	1392 - 1568
MOMOYAMA	1568 - 1600
EDO	1600 - 1868
MEIJI	1868 - 1912
TAISHŌ	1912 - 1926
SHŌWA	1926 present

This chronology is based on that which appears in the catalogue of *The Great Japan Exhibition*
© Royal Academy of Arts 1981.

ANDON KANBAN A paper-covered lampstand on which the name of the shop is written. Because they were perishable, few old examples remain.

IORI KANBAN A sign associated exclusively with the world of Kabuki theater. Sometimes referred to as *maneki* boards, these signs are inscribed with the name of a single Kabuki actor and placed in front of a theatre where he is performing. (Plate 104)

JITSUBUTSU KANBAN *Jitsubutsu* is defined as "a real thing, an actual object, beyond the natural life-size." Jitsubutsu kanban are signs which incorporate the actual object or use an enlarged version of it as the kanban. (Plate 62)

KANBAN The literal meaning of the compound is *kan*, "see" and *ban*, "board." It is the commonly accepted Japanese word for a shop sign. It is frequently pronounced and spelled with an "m" *(kamban)* for euphony. Although kanban are generally made of wood, the word also applies to signs of tin, paper and, occasionally, cloth.

MANEKI KANBAN *Maneki* means "invitation." These signs use well-known symbols, such as the beckoning cat, the *tanuki*, (badger) and Okame, Goddess of Mirth, to invite customers. Kabuki actors' name signs are also known as *maneki* boards. (Plate 1)

MOKEI KANBAN *Mokei* means "model" or "pattern." These are signs without writing in the shape of the object sold or which depict symbolically a service rendered. They are recognized by shape and do not require literacy for comprehension. (Plate 6)

MOZŌ KANBAN *Mozō* is literally, "dummy, oversized model, mock-up." This term can have a slightly derogatory tone. (Plate 37)

NIKAI KANBAN Literally, "second story signs", they are also known as *nikai yanekanban*. *Yane*, "roof," refers here to the architecture of the shop since these signs were prominently placed between the eaves of the first floor and the main roof of the building, to decorate the facade. Many consist of a long flat piece of wood, placed parallel to the main wall, so that while they are prominent, they can only be read from the front. (Plate 95)

NOBORI KANBAN Cloth banners bearing the name of the shop and hung top and side from a bamboo frame.

NOKIZURI KANBAN A compound of *noki* "eaves, along the eaves" and *tsurusu* "to suspend, hang as a chandelier," nokizuri kanban is used interchangeably for the phrase sage kanban, as both imply hanging from the eaves. *Nokizuri* particularly applies to hanging signs which consist of a single board with characters in relief. (Plate 58.)

NOREN The traditional cloth curtain which hangs in the doorway of many Japanese shops, announcing the name of the merchant or his service. (Figure 3)

ŌIRI KANBAN *Ōiri* means, literally, "a full house, capacity audience." These signs, traditionally written on a red and white banner, are a gesture of general welcome. When placed in front of a theatre, it means "all-sold out." (Plate 102)

SAGE KANBAN From the verb *sageru* meaning "to hang, hang out a sign, put up a signboard." These are signs which hang down from the eaves at street level and are the most common type of kanban. They often have side handles, making it easy to take them in each night. (Plate 72)

SHŌKEI KANBAN *Shōkei* refers to "elaboration" and these are the most decorative signs. Shōkei kanban are ornately and intricately decorated, painted or carved. (Plate 56)

YAKATA KANBAN *Yakata* literally means "mansion." These signs are the most architectural kanban. They were conceived as permanent constructions and were designed as part of the architectural plan. Often they hung at right angles to the building facade and were built into the second story roof. To insure harmony of style, they were usually made by a master carpenter rather than an ordinary sign-maker. (Plate 17)

YANE KANBAN *Yane* means "roof," so yane kanban are signs which have their own protective little roof. This explains how painted and even lacquered signs could survive years of exposure. Signs have often become separated from their roofs and one can only surmise that certain kanban once had them. (Plate 55)

YŌKI KANBAN *Yōki* means "receptacle or container." Yōki kanban are signs which identify the product by its container. They advertise common household necessities and are directed to a largely illiterate audience. (Plate 2)

GLOSSARY OF SHOPS AND OCCUPATIONS REFERRED TO IN THIS BOOK

(In Japanese, the suffix *ya* indicates a shop where a particular article is sold or made.)

Bunbōgu-ya–Stationery shop (contemporary)
Cha-ya–Tea shop, tea dealer, tea house
Chōmen-ya–Stationery shop, in olden times
Enogu-ya–Paint shop
Fude-ya–Brush shop
Furo-ya–Bathhouse
Furumono-ya–Bric-a-brac shop, shop for old things
Gakkiten–Music shop
Geta-ya–Clog maker, clog shop
Gofuku-ya–Shop for kimono and kimono fabric
Hasami-ya–Scissors shop
Hikite-ya–Maker of door pulls and door hardware
Hon-ya–Book store
Ichizen meshi-ya–Fast food shop serving rice dishes
Inrō-ya–*Inrō* (seal case) maker
Jōmae-ya–Locksmith
Kabuto-ya–Helmet maker
Kagami-ya–Mirror shop
Kami-ya–Shop for Japanese papers
Kanamono-ya–Hardware shop; ironmonger
Kasa-ya–Umbrella shop
Kashi-ya–Candy shop
Katsura-ya–Wig maker
Kiji-ya–Cloth shop
Kottōhin-ya–Antique shop
Kushi-ya–Comb shop
Kusuri-ya–Drug store
Kutsu-ya–Shoe maker
Manjū-ya–Dumpling shop
Megane-ya–Eyeglass shop
Meshi-ya–Fast food restaurant
Ningyō-ya–Doll shop
Nokogiri-ya–Saw maker
Oke-ya–Bucket shop
Omocha-ya–Toy shop
Rōsoku-ya–Candle shop
Ryōgae-ya–Money changer
Sakana-ya–Fish shop
Saka-ya–Sake brewer; sake shop; also sells *miso*
Saya-shi–Sword scabbard maker
Sembei-ya–Rice cracker shop
Sensu-ya–Fan shop
Shichi-ya–Pawnbroker
Shūri-ya–Repair shop
Somemono-ya–Textile dyer
Tabako-ya–Tobacconist
Tabi-ya–Japanese sock shop
Tako-ya–Kite shop
Tōfu-ya–Bean curd shop
Tokei shūri-ya–Watch repair shop
Yakkyoku–Pharmacy
Yao-ya–Greengrocer

BIBLIOGRAPHY

Selected Sources in English

BOOKS

Bushell, Raymond. *The Inrō Handbook.* Weatherhill, New York and Tokyo, 1979.

Chiba, Reiko. *The Seven Lucky Gods of Japan.* Charles E. Tuttle Co., Rutland, Vt., and Tokyo, 1966.

Dorson, Richard M. *Folk Legends of Japan.* Charles E. Tuttle Co., Rutland, Vt., and Tokyo, 1962.

Hauge, Victor and Takako. *Folk Traditions in Japanese Art.* International Exhibitions Foundation, Washington D.C. and Kodansha International, New York and Tokyo, 1979.

Henderson, Harold, and Louis Ledoux. *Sharaku.* E. Weyhe, New York, 1939.

Hibbett, Howard. *The Floating World in Japanese Fiction.* Grove Press, New York, 1960.

Hickman, Money and Peter Fetchko. *Japan Day by Day.* Peabody Museum of Salem, Salem, MA, 1977.

Hillier, J. *The Uninhibited Brush.* Hugh M. Moss, London, 1974.

Joly, Henri L. *Legend in Japanese Art.* 1908. Reprint. Charles E. Tuttle Co., Rutland, Vt., and Tokyo, 1967.

Kaempfer, Engelbert. *The History of Japan,* Volume 2, 1906. Reprint. AMS Press, New York, 1971.

Maeda, Mana. *Ji—Signs and Symbols of Japan.* Kodansha International, New York and Tokyo, 1975.

Morse, Edward S. *Japan Day by Day: 1877-79, 1882-85.* Houghton Mifflin, New York, 1917.

Norman, E. Herbert. *Andō Shōeki and the Anatomy of Japanese Feudalism.* Transactions of the Asiatic Society of Japan, Third Series, Volume 2. Tokyo, 1949.

Roberts, John G. *Mitsui.* Weatherhill, New York and Tokyo, 1973.

Robinson, B. W. *The Arts of the Japanese Sword.* Charles E. Tuttle Co., Rutland, Vt., 1961.

Rosenfield, John M., Fumiko E. Cranston, and Edwin A. Cranston. *The Courtly Tradition in Japanese Art and Literature.* Selections from the Hofer and Hyde Collections. Fogg Art Museum, Harvard University, Cambridge, 1973.

Sasaki, Jōhei. *Ōkyo and the Maruyama Shijō School of Japanese Painting.* St. Louis Art Museum, 1980.

Sheldon, Charles D. *Rise of the Merchant Class in Tokugawa Japan: 1600-1868.* 1958. Reprint. Russell and Russell, New York, 1973.

Sumiya, Mikio, and Kōji Taira. *An Outline of Japanese Economic History: 1603-1940.* University of Tokyo Press, Tokyo, 1979.

Watson, William, ed. *The Great Japan Exhibition: Art of the Edo Period, 1600-1868.* Royal Academy of the Arts, London, 1981.

Wilcox, R. Turner. *The Mode in Footwear.* Charles Scribner's Sons, New York, 1948.

Wilson, Eunice. *History of Shoes.* Sir Isaac Pitman and Sons, London, 1969.

Yanagi, Sōetsu. *The Unknown Craftsman.* Kodansha International, Tokyo and Palo Alto, Ca., 1972.

Yazaki, Takeo. *Social Change and the City in Japan.* Translated by D. L. Swain. Japan Publications Trading Co., San Francisco, 1968.

PERIODICALS AND BROCHURES

Bushell, Raymond. "*Kiseruzutsu:* The Japanese Pipe Case." Arts of Asia, Volume 10, No. 6 (November-December 1980), pp. 86-96.

Shiveley, Donald. "Sumptuary Regulations and Status in Early Tokugawa Japan." Asian Studies Bulletin, Volume 25, 1964-65.

Selected Sources in Japanese

BOOKS

Ehon Kanban Hinagata (Illustrations of Kanban Samples). Kyoto, 1730.

Endō, Takeshi, and Keitarō Miyamoto. *Nippon no Mingu* (Folk Implements of Japan). 4 Volumes. Tokyo Keiyusha, 1964-67.

Hayashi, Miichi. *Edo Kanban Zufu* (Pictures of Edo Kanban). Miki Shobō, Tokyo, 1977.

Matsumiya, Saburō. *Edo no Kanban* (Signboards of Edo). Tōhō Shobō, Tokyo, 1959.

Okitsu, Kaname. *Edo Shomin no Fūzoku to Ninjō* (Daily Life and Customs of the Common People in Edo). 3 Volumes. Ōfū-sha, Tokyo, 1979.

Takahashi, Masato. *Meiji no Shōka* (Meiji Trading Houses). Iwasaki Bijutsusha, Tokyo, 1981.

Yamazaki, Masao. *Nihon no Kanban* (Japanese Signboards). Marusha, Tokyo, 1978.

This book has been jointly planned and produced by JOHN WEATHERHILL, INC.
and THE JAPAN SOCIETY of New York.
Editorial supervision: LETITIA BURNS O'CONNOR.
Composition: CONTINENTAL TYPOGRAPHICS, Woodland Hills, California.
Engraving and printing of the plates in four color,
monochrome gravure and offset, and printing of the text: NISSHA, Kyoto.
Binding: MAKOTO, Tokyo.
The typeface used is GOUDY OLD STYLE, cap. initials are JEUNE.

ABOVE: The Weatherhill *kanban* which is mounted
outside the offices of John Weatherhill Inc., Tokyo. Designed by
Meredith Weatherby and executed by Sakazume Kanban, Tokyo.